SPAIN

Flamenco

Flamenco
Gypsy Dance and Music
from Andalusia

Edited by Claus Schreiner

With Essays by
Madeleine Claus, Christof Jung, Holger Mende,
Marion Papenbrok, Bernhard-Friedrich Schulze,
and Ehrenhard Skiera

Translated by
Mollie Comerford Peters

Reinhard G. Pauly,
General Editor

AMADEUS PRESS
Portland, Oregon

Fischer edition editorial advisor: Heide Kobert

The Amadeus edition translator wishes to thank Mrs. Ann Pfingsten for her help in rendering the cante coplas from Spanish.

German edition © 1985 Fischer Taschenbuch
Verlag GmbH,
Frankfurt am Main

Translation © 1990 by Amadeus Press
(an imprint of Timber Press, Inc.)
All rights reserved

ISBN 0-931340-25-X
Printed in Singapore

AMADEUS PRESS
9999 S.W. Wilshire
Portland, Oregon 97225

Library of Congress Cataloging-in-Publication Data

Flamenco. English.
   Flamenco : gypsy dance and music from Andalusia / edited by Claus
Schreiner ; with essays by Madeleine Claus ... [et al.] ; translated
by Mollie Comerford Peters ; Reinhard G. Pauly, general editor.
       p.   cm.
   Translation of: Flamenco.
   Includes bibliographical references and discography.
   ISBN 0-931340-25-X
   1. Flamenco--History and criticism.   I. Schreiner, Claus.
II. Claus, Madeleine. III. Pauly, Reinhard G. IV. Title.
ML3712.F613 1990
784.18'82--dc20   89-48450
                                                          CIP
                                                          MN

CONTENTS

Preface   7

Introduction, by Claus Schreiner   11
   Andalusia: Pena and Alegrina   11
   Gitanos or Gypsies   14
   The Geography of Flamenco   21
   The Art of Flamenco   22
   Juergas, Cabales, and Aficionados   27
   Cabales and Love—Flamenco Studies and the Public   28
   A New Era?   31

History of Flamenco, by Marion Papenbrok   35
   What Is Flamenco Anyway?   35
   History of the Romanichals   37
   Andalusia   37
   First References to Flamenco   42
   The "Golden Age" of Flamenco   43
   Decadence and Renaissance   45
   New Directions   47

The Spiritual World of Flamenco, by Marion Papenbrok   49

Cante Flamenco, by Christof Jung   57
   Periods/History   59
   Elements of the Cante   62
   Accompaniment to Cante   66
   Where the Cante Is Sung   67
   Styles of Cante   67
   The Cantaores   79

Baile Flamenco, by Madeleine Claus   89
   The Golden Age   89
   Origins   93
   Baile jondo   94
   Techniques of Baile Flamenco   97
   Styles of Baile   101
   La Joselito   103
   Bailaoras and Bailaores   113

Guitarra Flamenca, by Bernhard-Friedrich Schulze and
Ehrenhard Skiera   121
    Esthetics, History, and Construction of the Flamenco Guitar
        (Bernhard-Friedrich Schulze)   121
    Musical Forms and Techniques for the Flamenco Guitar
        (Ehrenhard Skiera)   136

Castanets and Other Rhythmic and Percussive Elements,
by Ehrenhard Skiera   147
    Castañuelas or Palillos   147
    Jaleo, Palmas, Pitos and Taconeo   151

Flamencos—Pictures and Notes from Andalusia,
by Holger Mende   153

Appendixes
    A. Flamenco Festivals   165
    B. Peñas ("Clubs") flamencas   166
    C. Flamenco Research Centers   166
    D. Suppliers of Sheet Music, Records, Books   167
    E. Flamenco Guitar Instruction Guides   167
    F. Addresses of Famous Flamenco Guitar Makers   168
    G. Discography   168
    H. Glossary   171

Bibliography   173

About the Authors   176

PREFACE

The rapid dissemination of pop and commercial music and its ubiquity has led to a noticeable reduction in the marvelous array of unique music idioms in the modern world. Pop music and its forum, "show business," are widely agreed to lack significant new ideas, stimuli, sounds and rhythms. Interestingly enough however, the voracious demand of producers and consumers alike could readily be satisfied by the exotic fare contained in the recipe book of "raw material" from cultures that, for either economic or political reasons, are unable to make their music known in an authentic manner outside their limited regional boundaries.

Now that the media, including electronic means of communication, allow such rapid exchanges of information, pop charts are read the world over the moment they are released. A show written for Las Vegas might also be seen simultaneously in Oslo or Kyoto. Millions are spent on packaging popular music records so that they can rapidly make the "hit parade" in many countries on every continent.

Those who prefer their cultural fare pure and authentic are left to their own devices—often a frustrating experience since such unique local or regional musical traditions are largely ignored in the media as "minority music." Further, it is often very difficult to obtain records, scores or books dealing with these musical gems, and companies are increasingly forced to appeal to a small, dwindling number of buyers.

When such traditional forms do enter the international circuit they are usually in a diluted, hardly recognizable form resulting from the "pre-packaging" of the music industry. The process of internationalizing such "raw materials" seems inevitably to reduce it to our own esthetic concepts. This kind of adaptation is nothing short of adulteration.

In the name of "world music," the obvious and identifiable characteristics of the unique musical forms and practices of many cultural traditions have been reduced to the highly stylized canons of pop music in order to extend the exploitation of the music industry.

Gypsy-Andalusian flamenco has particularly suffered from these practices. Flamenco is the music, dance and attitude towards life of a Spanish minority. And yet the Spanish themselves have contributed enormously to watering down and adulterating its pure forms. Yet how often does a country get a chance to greatly enhance its attractiveness by promoting a well known concept or slogan such as "flamenco?"

Under the headline "Matadors in the Heat of Passion," I recently read the following newspaper account:

> With the dust swirling from their gowns, the Spanish flamenco dancers, looking every bit like they were Meissen china dolls, twirled into the bright spotlights with a fascinating precision and angular, squared-off gestures. There was a white flash of legs—brief, chaste and innocent; there was smoke in the air. At the microphones were tough matadores of folkloristic flamenco song and rousing rhythmic clapping. In the heat of passion they proudly kept watch over their women as they wildly turned and twisted. . . . But a true Spaniard restrains his passion; eroticism becomes a well-calculated dancing figure, the control and squaring of feelings. In the background—in the pale light of a sparsely decorated stage—a few guitarists and a flute player fingered the usual rhythms and harmonic chord progressions, limiting themselves (one could almost call it an incredibly grand, abstract art of vague insinuation) to a few not particularly showy dabs of musical color and acknowledging only the archaic forces and sometimes grotesque ecstacy unfolding at the front of the stage.

The authors of this book have consciously distanced their views and writing about flamenco from this kind of "hype" which not only such writers but also the tourist boom in Spain have produced. Thus, the title *Flamenco: Gypsy Dance and Music from Andalusia* restricts our theme to the original flamenco of the Andalusian gypsies which in turn touches on the essence and origins of flamenco itself. In so saying the authors must acknowledge the fact that Gypsy-Andalusian flamenco is also performed outside Andalusia and that some great flamenco singers, dancers and guitarists are not gypsies.

The intimate knowledge of flamenco possessed by the authors derives in most cases from the very intimate associations they have formed with the gypsy world, which in turn understandably leads to some differing opinions of various flamenco artists. After all, this kind of subjective judgment goes on even in flamenco circles!

The adjective "puro" (pure) is a given among flamenco insiders both in Spain and elsewhere. But such slavish devotion to an ideal of flamenco is somewhat anachronistic, for after 1782 many flamenco artists and flamenco styles came from a non-gypsy world. Moreover, flamenco initiates have long complained that the younger *cantaores* do not sing pure flamenco. Furthermore, many Spanish gypsies paid no heed to flamenco. Clearly all the talk about purity seems a bit exaggerated.

Lastly, we must admit that even "impure" forms of flamenco can possess a sense of beauty and skill that are very pleasing. So, the distancing we have in mind primarily concerns those numerous performances that style themselves "flamenco" while knowingly offering an adulterated product.

Christof Jung, one of the authors, advised me shortly before the manuscript was completed that Gypsy-Andalusian flamenco has "almost no chance." The last great cantaor whom he heard, Agujetas, could sing martinetes one after the other for eight hours on end. Where could one find such a master today among Gypsy-Andalusian flamenco performers? As a traditionalist he fears for the imminent demise of this gypsy art form; in his words, there are too many gypsies "who no longer have any hunger in their voices."

This book is intended to offer only a basic introduction to Gypsy-Andalusian flamenco. Its authors are conscious of the fact that their essays cannot be a substitute for the thorough research and publishing by Spanish flamencologists. We therefore strongly urge readers seeking more detailed information to consult the writings listed in the bibliography.

Is flamenco a dying art? For anyone fortunate enough to have recently attended a good *tablao* or a private *juerga* and witnessed the present vitality of *arte flamenco*, the answer to this question is, to my way of thinking, obvious.

I wish to extend my gratitude to the authors, none of whom refused my request to write an essay. I particularly thank Bernhard Schulze for his critical suggestions, and Detlev Eberwein, Hermjo Klein and Jose El Bigote for their suggestions and advice. I especially would like to have asked Olaf Hudtwalcker for a contribution, but unfortunately he passed away on April 23, 1984 in Barcelona. He loved art, jazz and flamenco.

Claus Schreiner

Diego Vargas

INTRODUCTION

Claus Schreiner

Andalusia: Pena and Alegria

For thousands of years, peoples from Europe, the Near East and North Africa ventured into the southern part of Western Europe now known as Spain. Celts, Phoenicians, Greeks, Carthaginians, Romans, Vandals, Visigoths and Moors all joined the original inhabitants of the Iberian Peninsula. All penetrated to the southern part of the peninsula, then called "Vandalusia" by the Moors, despite the fact that the Vandals had been driven into North Africa by the Visigoths in 429 A.D. Beginning in the 7th century, Arabs from Algeria and Morocco, enlisted by the Visigoths to help in their struggles against King Roderick, penetrated deeply into the Iberian Peninsula, as far north as southern France. Yet the northern part of the peninsula still contained a few Christian kingdoms that had for centuries endeavored to regain the lands controlled by the Arabs, in what came to be known as the *reconquista:* Castile, Aragon, Leon, Navarra and even Portugal.

As the troops of Castile and Aragon were besieging the gates of Granada (the last bastion of the Moors), Christopher Columbus was waiting impatiently near the coast for the queen's permission to set sail for the Indies. Shortly thereafter the "new world," the *conquista,* with all its concomitant horrors of slavery, genocide and suppression, brought with it the seeds of a Latin-American culture.

Andalusia was at this time already an ethno-cultural melting pot. The cities, in particular, had been strongly influenced culturally by the Phoenicians, Greeks, Visigoths and Moors. Even before the coming of the Moors, Isidor, the Bishop of Seville, had produced a substantial encyclopedia, and Rekkeswind wrote the *Lex Visigothorum,* which helped create a sense of Spanish identity and nationalism. During the period of the Moorish caliphates and monarchies, Cordoba blossomed into a city of almost a million inhabitants. The Alhambra and the buildings of the Alcazar still bear witness to the flowering of Granada, Cádiz and Seville under Moorish rule.

Wheat and olive trees had already been cultivated around Betis (Guadalquivir) by the Romans, who shipped agricultural products to Rome from the province of Baetica. The Visigoths and Moors continued to cultivate the countryside around Guadalquivir, Genil and Guadiana. The hope of restoring Christian rule in Andalusia may well have been only one of the reasons why northern Spanish royal houses supported the *reconquista,* for they could not help but envy the wealth of Moorish Spain.

Five hundred years later, Andalusia remains a thorn in the side of the government in Madrid. Unemployment is high; the exodus of people from the region (over a million in the 1970s alone) to other large cities in Spain is staggering. Even the annual vacation pilgrimages by central Europeans to the tourist resorts of Málaga and Torremolinos are not an undiluted benefit to the region.

Andalusia has always been a land of extremes. In the north the natural boundary is formed by the mountain slopes of the Sierra Morena, in the east by the snow-covered peaks of the Sierra Nevada, and east of that by the barren Sierra de Gador. In the south the region is defined by the Costa del Sol and Costa de Luz, the Mediterranean and the Atlantic Ocean. Cork (oak) tree forests, vineyards and olive plantations border the arid Sierras.

No doubt a sense of "nevertheless," a defiance in the face of "pena andaluza" (Andalusian suffering), has contributed to the Andalusian saying "poder andaluz" (Andalusian fortitude). It is seen and sensed in the poverty which exists side by side with abundance and wealth, the caves and wretched cottages near villas and palaces, in the gardens in bloom everywhere beside the asphalt wastelands of the tourist resorts.

But these contrasts do not qualify Andalusia as an exotic enclave in Europe—its history is devoid of any such romanticism. Here too, aggression and religious hatred have led to persecution of the Jews, deportations, inquisitions, and political persecution of minorities: Arabs, Jews and gypsies.

But by way of contrast there is the "alegria Andaluza," the *joie de vivre* exhibited by the Andalusian people in their large number of fiestas and *romerias* (church fairs). Even pilgrimages, feast days and Holy Week are celebrated with noisy, energetic festivities. The church calendar, which the church early synchronized with "pagan" rites and customs, is the social calendar. Carnival begins on Epiphany; masquerades and *vaquillas* take place on the feast of St. Sebastian; water rites, solstice celebrations and maypole festivals are tied to spring and summer feast days. In mid-September, *Despescas* is celebrated in the saltworks at Cádiz; in neighboring Jeres de la Frontera they celebrate *Vendimias* (grape harvest festivals); and in Huelva, in August, the people commemorate Columbus' voyage with *Colombiana.*

And music is an integral part of all these celebrations. Andalusia is the home of the *fandango,* whose origins are still unexplained. Like the Andalusian *cartagenera, morisca, granaina, minera, murciana, rondena* and *taranta,* the fandango is often attributed to the cultural traditions of the Moors. By the early 18th century, dances called the fandango had appeared in the New World from Santo Domingo to Argentina. The Africans, Indians and mestizos living in the Americas changed it, interweaving it with the patterns of their own dance rituals. Since the Andalusian ports of Cádiz and Huelva had long been the gateway to the New World of Latin America, the theory that the fandango was re-imported from Latin America back into Andalusia has been advanced by numerous commentators.

The *malagueñas* are a part of the Andalusian group of fandangos. In the late Middle Ages, jugglers and minstrels brought the Spanish romance to Andalusia. Under Moorish influence, the Zéjel (Arabic Zayal) song form developed, named after Zyriab, the "black nightingale," who introduced Arabic songs into Cordoba.

The *seguidillha,* in 3/4 time, was also brought from Castile to Andalusia, where it became the *sevillana.* The Spanish *bolero* is a hybrid dance between these sevillanas and elements of the Spanish *contradanza.*

The *jota,* which in Andalusia was interwoven with Andalusian folk music, also originated in old Castile. But the antecedents of the many dances that made their appearance in Andalusia in the 16th and 17th centuries remain murky: the *sarabanda, zarambeque, chacona, gayumba, zambapalo, paracumbe* and the *guineo.* It is thought that they were influenced by North African and black African dances (*morisca*).

Granada

Even before the conquest of Latin America and the opening of the slave trade to the New World, slaves of African origin were not uncommon on the Iberian Peninsula. This fact has given rise to speculation that Moorish songs and dances, combined with Celtic folk music and the folk music of the Visigoths in Andalusia, were modified by Africans living there and exported to Latin America. There their songs and dances were further transformed by African slaves and brought back to Andalusia by travelers and returning emigrants. Writers like Lope de Vega and Cervantes characterized them as imports "from the Indies." Whatever their beginnings, all these songs and dances have long since evolved into other forms and can no longer be distinguished nor identified. Nevertheless, their evolution in Latin America may account for the ease with which Latin American dances and songs like the bolero, milonga, guajira, rumba and colombiana were so readily accepted by Andalusians in the 19th and 20th centuries.

The most striking feature of many Andalusian dances is the *zapateado*, or foot stamping, and the *jaleo*, an encouraging call.

But above all, Andalusia is the home of flamenco.

Gitanos or Gypsies

According to Rüdiger Vossen, between 250,000 and 700,000 gypsies are now living in Spain: *Gitanos Béticos, Gitanos Catalanes, Gitanos Castellanos, Gitanos Extremeños, Cafeletes* and *Hungaros*. The term Gitanos Béticos refers directly to the Andalusian gypsies, of whom the majority have lived as *Gitanos Caseros* (= not nomadic) for generations. The Andalusian gypsies are Calé (calé = black man) and consciously keep their distance from the Hungaros (or Romanies) and the Sinti.

The Gitanos Béticos, with their distinct familial lineages, clans and ancestry, also have their own social structure and live in close-knit societies. Yet they also think of themselves as Andalusians, though they never openly articulate this sentiment in their cante flamenco or through patriotic gestures. Ricardo Molina, an authority on flamenco, however, justifiably points out that a kind of patriotism and declaration of loyalty to Andalusia is to be found in those parts of the cante which speak tenderly of the gypsies' immediate surroundings (R. Molina, *Obra Flamenca*, p. 57).

> In my beautiful Andalusia
> Huelva is the best,
> How beautiful her women
> How charming the bay
> And what wonderful fandangos it has.
> (fandango)

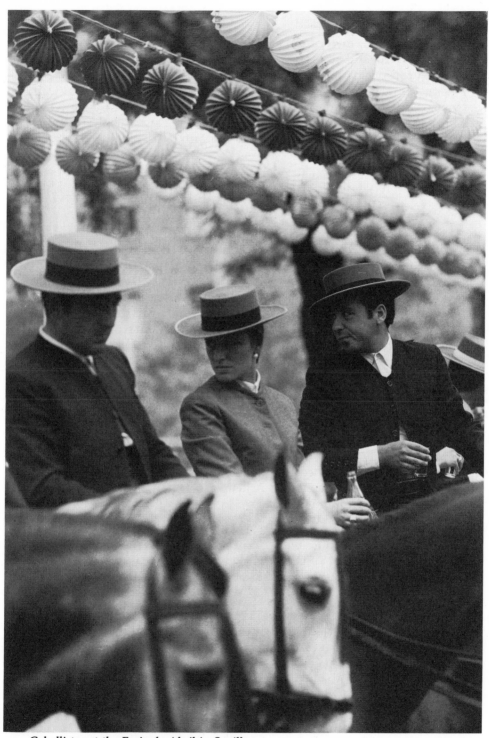

Caballistas at the Feria de Abril in Seville

In any case, love of the earth and nature is deeply rooted in the gypsy psyche and soul which distinguishes them from the *payos*, the non-gypsies, from whom they consciously distance themselves. In his classic work *El Arte Flamenco*, Donn E. Pohren quotes an old gypsy: "The poor payos don't understand that we are the last sons of God and that they are slaves to a system that reduces their life to meaninglessness. . . . We symbolize everything they lack: integrity, individuality, freedom" (Pohren, p. 21).

> Though I wear Spanish clothes
> I was born a gypsy.
> I like being a gypsy
> And have no desire to be a Spaniard.
> (tonás)

Spaniards (payos), for their part, generally distrust gypsies and view them as an immoral and uneducated people.

But living out of doors in the arms of nature no longer typifies today's Andalusian gypsies. Only a small handful of them still live as nomads, maintaining the old traditions. Most of them have adapted the lifestyle of the payos. Because farmwork pays so little, and because living in scattered, nomadic settlements in the countryside fails to satisfy the gypsy's need for togetherness, the majority have settled near the big cities. Living in close-knit enclaves near the city center permits them to earn a livelihood working in the *tabernas*. Gypsy barrios are found on the outskirts of the major cities of Baja-Andalusia (southern Andalusia), including Seville, Jerez and Cádiz. As early as the 19th century, Triana outside Seville was a major *gitanería* having a decisive role in the development of flamenco gitano-andaluz. Many gypsies remain a part of the underprivileged class of Andalusian society; poor and with few educational opportunities, they live in the slums of the barrios.

> In Triana it is said
> in no uncertain terms,
> if you're born a caló
> You'd better get used to suffering.
> (debla)

At the heart of their social organization are the family and the clan. A gypsy's relationship with his extended family ends only with death. Eternal loyalty to the clan and support of clan members are fundamental unwritten laws in gypsy society. The clan leader is extraordinarily powerful, and all the members of the clan defer to his decisions. His authority also extends to determining inter-clan relationships; whether permitted or, due to a feud, forbidden. Weddings have a special significance for gypsies. Pohren's gypsy boasts: "We are the only ones who really know how to celebrate marriage." Weddings usually last

at least three days, with the bride as the centerpiece. She is "kidnapped," examined to see if she is still a virgin, and finally, surrounded by the members of her clan, performs an involved wedding dance.

The gypsies have an elaborate code of honor dictating every detail of correct social behavior. Thus, for example, a flamenco artist is given no greater respect than an honorable gypsy merchant or shopkeeper. But in both cases it is expected that, once their familial needs are met, they share their earnings with the needy of their clan. (Flamenco artists receive anywhere from 30,000 to 200,000 pesetas for a performance. The impresario, J. A. Pulpon, annually publishes a breakdown of performers' earnings; Fosforito, Lebrijano, Menese, El Cabrero and Camaron de la Isla are among the highest paid cantaores. Smaller fees are paid for Andalusian flamenco *peñas* than for performances outside Andalusia.) Cleanliness and a neat appearance are *de rigueur*. Long-haired, bearded tourists dressed in casual clothes, traveling to Andalusia to hear gypsy-Andalusian flamenco, and to befriend the gypsies, do not exactly meet gypsy expectations.

Nomadic Andalusian gypsies live a hand to mouth existence. To quote Pohren's gitano again: "Just to work—like the payos—to earn money or prestige, or to get ahead, or whatever. This is the great virtue of the gypsies; we refuse to throw away our integrity like that." Traditionally gypsies have held jobs as blacksmiths, bartenders, or helping out around the bullfighting rings. In addition, they now work as horse traders, waiters (or other service industry jobs), musicians, flamenco singers and dancers, and bullfighters. The members of virtually every clan now hold such jobs, but foremost among their ranks are those whose members become flamenco artists and bullfighters. Of all the clans, it is the "flamenco dynasties" which have become famous, the Cortes and Amayas from Cordoba or the Ortegas from Cádiz.

Despite these differences, the Andalusian gypsies have much in common with Andalusian payos. In addition to *machismo* and patriarchy, both revere the feminine: Mother Earth and the Mother of God. So the spring festivals recalling the ancient fertility cycle and worship of the Virgin take on a special meaning in Andalusia. Although the gypsies have adopted the Christianity of the payos, they prefer a specifically gypsy image of the Mother of God in their worship. Not only do gypsies take part in Holy Week processions, but saeta singers like Maria Vargas or El Lebrijano are indispensable. All flamenco performances are suspended during Holy Week.

> Behold the brown-skinned Christ,
> Lord of the gypsies,
> The highest and holiest,
> With His hands bound,
> Poor Jesus of Nazareth.
> (saeta)

Hardly any Andalusian festival would be complete without its gypsy flamenco performances: *carnaval,* feast days of patron saints, *romerias,* and *juergas.* In the summer months, many gypsy clans travel from festival to festival to earn their living by singing, dancing, trading, etc. So common is this practice that many *tabernas* have put a stop to it by posting signs in their bars reading "No singing, dancing or hand clapping."

The gypsies also share the Andalusian's love of bullfighting (a payo tradition). In many respects, bullfighting reflects the emotional world of the gypsies. Life with all its stresses, challenges and difficulties, death, survival and resurrection, are metaphysical and spiritual concerns common to both the bullfight and flamenco which awaken similar responses in their audiences. *Toro, cante* and *gitano baile* share, according to Climent, a similar way of viewing, sensing and making use of the world. He interprets some of the figures danced by the *bailaores* as similar to those used by matadors and observes that cantaores singing siguiriyas follow the movements made with *muleta.* In commercial flamenco presentations, this bullfighting aspect is commonly exaggerated. A gypsy cantaor is seen as a *cantaor de verdad* (singer of truth), and in the moment when the matador either clearly kills the bull or clumsily, fearfully and hesitantly butchers it, a moment of truth emerges for him as a man. The wine of Andalusia also plays a strong role in flamenco and gypsy life. The grape-growing regions of Jerez and Rio Tinto have traditionally supplied the substance required by both the *cantaor* and his audience to express *jipío* (laments, sobs). But here too, as gypsies have been assimilated into Andalusian payos' ways, they have turned to cognac and whiskey.

And the gypsies share with the payos of the Andalusian cities the same mass culture of the cities of the world: Disco music, jogging, fashion fads, mass media—all part of a shared contemporary life.

> Lord Mayor,
> Don't bother putting the thieves in jail,
> For you have a daughter
> Who steals hearts.
> (petenera)

Payos not only regard gypsies with suspicion but deny gypsy-Andalusian flamenco as a distinctive art form within Andalusian culture.

The Spanish Andalusians argue that in the absence of Andalusia's cultural diversity and the tradition of Andalusian music imbedded in it, there would be no flamenco. The payos feel that they are co-authors of this tradition. Moreover, they argue that they were the first to recognize the attraction of flamenco not only to themselves but to others as well. These observations have some merit, for gypsy-Andalusian flamenco could not have developed independently out of the gypsy tradition. As a consequence of these views, Andalusian payos are aficionados and some have become notable flamenco performers. Since at least the period of the *cafés cantantes* (see the next chapter), numerous payo flamenco artists have emerged and for over 100 years, payos and gypsies have accepted the presence of the other.

Gypsy-Andalusian flamenco has in the course of time become very well known in other regions of Spain. But aside from the capital city of Madrid in Castile and Barcelona in Catalonia, flamenco has been unable to gain a foothold in Spain. The aversion to flamenco felt by some Andalusian payos is even more widely and powerfully felt in other regions of Spain. This unique form of song and dance is still looked down upon by many Spaniards. The middle class, which made a smooth transition from the "zarzuelas" to modern opera and ballet, has in Caballero Bonald's words been the "traditional enemy" of flamenco.

> Worker, why are you working?
> What you earn is not for you,
> To the rich it brings profit,
> To your family only grief.
> (cartagenera)

Gypsies in Barcelona

The Geography of Flamenco

Flamenco had its beginnings in southern Andalusia. Recent studies have concluded that the triangle of the cities of Cádiz, Ronda and Triana/Seville, with Jerez de la Frontera at their center, is the geographical birthplace of the early forms of *cante flamenco.*

But even within this triangular nexus the differing processes of acculturation between gypsy culture and local Andalusian traditions led to different flamenco forms. Seville and Cádiz remain today unsurpassed in the richness of their cante flamenco forms. Soleares, siguiriyas, bulerías, and cantes *a palo seco* are common to both these flamenco centers. Fandangos, tangos de Triana, and sevillanas, as well as the Andalusian folk music largely uninfluenced by gypsy music (the cantes camperos), are typical of the province of Seville. According to Pohren, alegrias, mirabras, romeras, caracoles, cantinas, tangos and tientos are more typical of flamenco in the province of Cádiz. Despite these differences the major flamenco centers in these provinces are: Triana, Osuna, Morón de la Frontera, Utrera and Lebrija in Seville province; and Jerez, Cádiz, Algeciras, Santa Maria and Arcos de la Frontera in Cádiz province. As gypsy-Andalusian flamenco exerted an increasingly more powerful influence on Andalusian folk music, its range expanded to the provinces of Huelva, Cordoba, Jaen, Málaga and Granada. But these are areas where Andalusian folk music is called "aflamencada," indicating its received nature. Despite the fact that flamenco appears in the local festivals and tablaos (see appendix) of the larger Andalusian cities outside the provinces of Seville and Cádiz, the geographical range of gypsy-Andalusian flamenco has remained essentially unchanged.

More than simple ignorance may have led Spaniards of other regions, such as Catalonia and Castile, to imitate gypsy-Andalusian flamenco: by sapping the cante of its authentic function, i.e. the union of singer and song, they also devalued its content. Cante flamenco reflects a constant search for shared feelings, which the interpreter then expresses on behalf of his audience. Gypsy-Andalusian flamenco was watered down with the introduction of popular songs and tourist spectaculars, and incorporated into a kind of national Spanish repertoire. A similar fate was suffered by other song forms as a result of cultural adaptation: The blues of the North American Negro, the *milongas* and *payadas* of the rural *payadores* on the La Plata, and the samba of the Morros from Rio.

Manuel de Falla, while in Paris, introduced Debussy and Ravel to Spanish guitar music and in particular flamenco guitar music. By about the mid-19th century, Rimsky-Korsakov and Mikhail Glinka had visited Cádiz and Granada. Georges Bizet had apparently never been to Spain when he wrote *Carmen,* having taken his inspiration from a *polo* by Manuel Garcia of Andalusia and Yradier's habanera *La Paloma* (Cuban habanera from Mexico).

This growing interest by serious composers, both in and outside of Spain, in adapting flamenco forms to art music, only served to further dilute it. Opera, zarzuela and ballet adopted various style characteristics of flamenco. Even performances by the Spanish National Ballet are far removed from any authentic flamenco tradition.

The Art of Flamenco

Gypsy-Andalusian flamenco had its roots in the gypsy musical tradition of southwestern Andalusia. As a persecuted and undesirable minority, the gypsies' only hope of survival was to adapt over time to the broad outlines of the culture of the dominant payos. However, they were able to protect the music of their culture by melding their traditional songs and dances with those of the prevailing Mozarabic culture.

Helped along by the gifted artistry of the gypsies, music and dance forms of the two traditions merged into what became known as flamenco gitano-andaluz or gypsy-Andalusian flamenco. Though the Calé songs repeatedly recount the oppressive conditions forcing this acculturation, the cante and its lyrics allowed them to maintain their freedom of personal expression in a "grito desgarrado" (heart-rending cry).

> If I could pour all my pain
> Into the streams,
> The water in the sea
> Would rise to the heavens.
> (soleares by Joaquin de Paula)

The authenticity of flamenco no longer depends upon whether it is performed by a gypsy or by a payo. As Pepe El de la Matrona, the great payo cantaor, has remarked, "it is not important to know if you are a payo or a gitano but to know how to sing and nothing else" (p. 226). All that matters is a common respect for authentic gypsy-Andalusian flamenco.

Whether to classify flamenco as folk music or not is a difficult question, despite its many features suggestive of such a typology: The close ties between origins; intrepreter; form of presentation and audience; performance suited only to an intimate setting; and the impossibility of commercializing it in its pure form. On the other hand, such a classification is only meaningful if flamenco possesses another crucial attribute of folklore best described as "constant development and change." Despite the widely differing personal styles of flamenco artists and the

Caraestaca

latitude of interpretation from one performance to the next, flamenco is deeply rooted in strict, formal traditions. In addition, it has long been the practice to speak of flamenco *artists*—a term rarely used when discussing folk music.

Since it has never enjoyed a mass audience and because its popular success is difficult to measure, flamenco cannot be classified as popular music either. Rather than thunderous applause by a large crowd, flamenco seeks direct communication with a small group, in which each individual comes to feel that he is being personally addressed.

Getting back to the term "artist": What the performers produce must then be "art"—*El Arte Flamenco.* These words describe an art form that, according to Pepe El de la Matrona, is fed from two sources: joy and sorrow. Soul and body must be in perfect harmony: intelligence governs the voice, heart conveys the content (Pepe de la Matrona, p. 223).

The gypsies turned to their own language to describe the key elements of Arte Flamenco. A singer is called a *cantaor* (Spanish: *cantor* or *cantador*, folk singer) and his song the *cante* (not *canto*). *Bailaor* and *bailaora* are the male and female flamenco dancers. Finally, the guitar player is called the *tocaor* (Spanish general usage: *tocador* or *guitarrista*). They use other terms too, such as *palillos* for castanets, rather than the Spanish *castanuelas*.

El Arte Flamenco is made up of three basic components:

> Cante (song)
> Baile (dance)
> Toque (guitar)

Those who have only been introduced to flamenco by one of the many performances given by touring flamenco troupes outside of Spain are surprised to learn that cante is the centerpiece of El Arte Flamenco. The cantaores in these commercial productions perform very much in the background and their singing is usually perceived as mere musical accompaniment to the dancers. Throughout its history, however, gypsy-Andalusian flamenco has been based on the pure art of singing, the cantaor often providing his own rhythmic accompaniment with no more than a style-stick (a *palo seco*). The guitar was introduced to accompany the song at the beginning of the 19th century, and only after that were dancers added.

Cantes, unlike Spanish *canciones,* French *chansons* and other song traditions, have neither refrains nor a constant rhythm, which makes them more difficult for a larger audience to identify and sing along with. Common themes include love, death, fate, morality, religion, social status, humor, people, honor, the stars and supernatural powers. When sung as *jondo* or *grande,* the cante expresses a collective feeling through one individual. But most typically the words turn on the personal experiences and sentiments of the singer. "The cantaor tries to convey his personal story to a few genuine witnesses" (Caballero Bonald, p. 53). He almost always writes his own lyrics, though in some few cases may use another singer's cante, altering it to fit his own perceptions. A specific singer's choice depends on his ability to express himself with music and lyrics: "You can never," says Climent, "suffer in the same way as another cantaor." This means that cante flamenco is less a standard formula of singing than a form that has always been inseparable from its singers. The particular style in which a cantaor sings can be so powerful and personal that it is thereafter associated with his name. Cantes are also named for their geographic origins, for example "por Cádiz" and "por Triana." When a cantaore dies, his song dies with him. Yet his art survives in the memory and in the work of other flamenco artists, aficionados and *cabales* (connoisseurs).

Climent divides cantaores into three general categories: the aesthetes, who concentrate on the formal aspects of cante (e.g. Pepe Marchena, Juanita Valderama); the flamencos, where the singer and song are in absolute accord (e.g. Pastora Pavón, Aurelio de Cádiz); and the individualists like José Palanca and Pepe Suarez (Climent, p. 137). Flamenco artists, particularly the cantaores and dancers, possess no formal training. They are self-taught, learning from the practices of their associates and predecessors. Contemporary gypsy-Andalusian flamenco is witnessing some new and differing trends. To the familiar historical periods (primitive phase, *flamenquismo,* neo-flamenco, post-flamenco and *Renascimiento*), recent scholars have added a neo-classical period (beginning in 1956), and, according to Agustin Gomez, also *mairenismo.* The latter movement was named after cantaor Antonio Mairena, who closely followed the tradition of his predecessors, stating that contemporaries had taught him nothing, that he had learned everything from the old masters (Gomez, p. 47). The guitarist Manolo El Caracol, who Gomez says originated *caracolismo,* is trying to separate himself completely from the concepts (see below) established by Garcia Lorca and Manuel de Falla, preferring to work outside any historical or scholarly reference to flamenco.

The art of flamenco with its cante, baile and toque would be incomplete without the *jaleos* (shouts) and *palmas* (hand clapping), contributed by the audience. The "ay's" create the unique climate in which the cante proceeds. Cries like "Por dios!" and "Eso es!" are affirmations and words of encouragement. Finger snapping (*pitos*) or rapping on the table are resorted to instead of or in addition to *palmas.*

El Arte Flamenco is further characterized by: Voice modulation (rich in melismas), various meters (3/4, 6/8, 7/8, 5/8, 1/4, and 2/4), improvisation, and to some extent *zapateo* (foot stamping) which first entered gypsy-Andalusian flamenco with the baile and was probably borrowed from Andalusian folk music. The terms "zapatero" and "zapateria" used by flamenco performers and aficionados, indicate that artists specializing in zapateado are a breed apart.

And finally there is the *duende* (demon), about which much has been written, but to which very little actual thought has been given. For instance, Garcia Lorca wrote: "Angel and muse come from outside; the angel brings light (= inspiration), the muse form ... But the demon (duende) has to be roused from the innermost reaches of the blood. We have to drive away the angel, banish the muse and overcome the fear of the scent of violets, exuded by 18th-century poetry, and fear of the mighty telescope in whose lenses the muse sleeps, sick of her confinement" (Lorca, *Teoria y juego del duende*).

Even so articulate a flamenco artist as Juan F. Talegas was only able to give his questioner this unsatisfying answer when queried about duende: "Nonsense! Where did you foreigners ever get this idea of duende? From Garcia Lorca maybe? Duende, it's like a fever, like malaria. I had the duende only twice in my life, but afterwards they had to carry me out" (Flamenco Studio, July, 1972).

Duende has been called the demon that puts flamencos in a trance. But the very nature of *cante jondo* contradicts all trance theories. We know, for instance, from trance states induced by mediums in Afro-American culture, that a stammered singsong may be possible, but certainly not the intellectual-emotional exertion of body and soul required by cante jondo.

It has also been said that demons are the spirits of dead gypsies. This may be an extension of the gypsy belief, documented by T. San Roman, that children who have died unbaptized are duendes. Bernhard-Friedrich Schulze has advanced a theory about duende which I find extremely useful. Duende, he says, is the agreement between an inner hearing and external sound. When what the cantaor feels in his soul and has translated into song in his inner ear, is identical with what is actually sung, he is overwhelmed with a feeling of achievement akin to a state of ecstasy. The same can be said of baile and toque artists. Artists in other genres have described nearly identical experiences. Schulze's views closely parallel Donn E. Pohren's, namely that virtuosity alone does not make a flamenco artist: "but it is imperative that he have the ability to identify with the duende, who is life-giving, and to impart this emotion or set of emotions to his public" (Pohren *El arte del Flamenco*, p. 43).

Juergas, Cabales, and Aficionados

While gypsy-Andalusian flamenco is to a large extent a solitary art, it nonetheless requires at least one person to either see it or hear it, someone to whom the "message" can be imparted and who in turn offers assent and encouragement.

Ricardo Molina gives us the following road map to flamenco: *La venta* (rural inn), *el cortijo* (manor), *la fonda* (bar), *el café, la calle* (street), *la taberna, la plaza* and *el jardin* (garden). At one time flamenco would have been performed quite typically in the *casa calé*—a gypsy home, cottage or cave. Gradually, however, it moved from the countryside, with its gardens and courtyards, to the city. There it was performed on the streets and in the plazas, then in the bars and nightclubs and finally, after 1922, at festivals held in concert halls and theaters.

Family celebrations, festivals in honor of the village patron saint or as part of the fertility cycle, feast days of the Church, and above all *juergas* and *reuniones*, those spontaneous happenings in intimate settings—all provide venues for flamenco performances. A juerga, which may be planned or unplanned, might begin on the street, somewhere in the countryside, or in the late afternoon or evening in a bar and often will not end until late the next day.

A juerga begins with eating and drinking, with wine and olives, and is embellished with tales from the world of flamenco. The older men talk about the past, describing and praising the virtues of this or that cantaore or tocaore. Someone starts singing to illustrate his point, whereupon another reaches for his guitar and increases the excitement by playing phrases associated with other guitarists. Then come the cantes, light and cheerful at first (*por bulerías*), followed by more serious ones. Cantaors involved in a juerga know when the time is right for them to strike up their cante, or they may wait to be asked to sing a certain cante. The juerga is still the best means of conveying the essence of flamenco for there is no separation here between audience and performer as there is between producer and consumer. Everyone takes part in the event in some way and supports each person performing. Flamencos and aficionados take turns shouting encouraging "ay's" or respond by calling out words of support and encouragement while supporting the performers with rhythmic hand clapping. Such behavior roughly corresponds to an audience exclaiming "Yeah, man!" to a blues song, or shouting an approving "Falou!" to the *sambistas* in Brazil. The atmosphere and comaraderie are much like that of a southern American gospel service.

Alcohol is usually consumed, but in moderation. Wine, whiskey and cognac relax the flamencos and aficionados. Molina says of alcohol: "Without this precious communion, there could be no cante."

The best audience for gypsy-Andalusian flamenco is not one

watching from a row of theater seats. Rather it is one whose members like an intimate setting, a shared experience, in which someone sings, dances or plays for them vicariously. These are the aficionados and *cabales*. Aficiaonados are flamenco insiders, the knowledgeable followers of the art. For absolute buffs Climent coined the term *cabales*, short for *aficionados cabales*. A *cabal* knows more than an aficionado, he knows how it feels ("sabe sentir").

Thus a *juerga flamenca* almost attains the qualities of a ritual, a ceremony of religious proportions. This is also why so much is said of "the initiated," as if one must go through an initiation in order to be received into the circle of *cabales*. The intimate space in which flamenco is usually performed gave the Franco regime no grounds for routine censorship of the cantes. The songs simply had no mass appeal. (There were a few isolated examples of political lyrics being banned during the Franco years, particularly those of Pepe el de la Matrona (see p. 46).

In its "Orden Jonda", the Cátedra de Flamencologia in Jerez selects the *Damas y Caballeros Cabales* of the year from among flamenco artists, persons involved with the bullfight, and Andalusian writers and artists. To be chosen, one must have been born in Andalusia and have contributed in some fashion to the renown of the Andalusian people (*jondos*). Public employees are not eligible.

Cabales and Love—Flamenco Studies and the Public

Cabales and aficionados are not confined to gypsies. They come from all socio-economic groups: Merchants, clerks, civil servants, politicians, etc. According to Pepe el de la Matrona, there were even some from the nobility among them who occasionally would contribute a few pesetas.

The composer Manuel de Falla, from Cádiz (1876–1946), and the poet Federico Garcìa Lorca (1898–1936), from Granada, were both aficionados. Lorca was one of the great proponents of *gitanismo*. He was the first to write down cante lyrics and even composed some of his own verse in cante style (*El Romancero Castellano, Romancero Gitano*, etc.). But R. Molina contends that Lorca depended upon some outmoded and erroneous assessments of flamenco (p. 74), in that he distinguished between cante jondo and flamenco by classifying the former as *cante primitivo andaluz*. Lorca's belief in the "alma musica" of the people probably clouded his judgment about the true origins of flamenco.

Manuel de Falla, Lorca's contemporary, explored flamenco music and incorporated some of its features into many of his compositions; e.g. his opera *La Vida Breve*, 1923; his ballet *Gitano*, 1915; and *Fantasia Bética*, 1919. Lorca and de Falla joined in the founding of the Centro Artistico in

Granada, which is dedicated to cante jondo. In 1922 they produced the first "Concurso de Flamenco" in Granada. In retrospect Molina is less than enthusiastic about this historic event because it turned out to be a festival for intellectuals, without the participation of the true masters of cante (Pastorà Pavón, for instance, was not there).

Lorca's *flamenquismo* had little influence on other Spanish poets, as they had long since come to view flamenco with disfavor. Even Ortega y Gasset, who so admired the bullfight, was little impressed by flamenco. Before the Granada fiasco, it was not just the *cafés cantantes* that were drawing people to flamenco. Opera and ballet companies gratefully lapped up this new art form from Andalusia, despite the fact that the strict forms and conventions of these two genres made it impossible to perform flamenco with any authenticity.

About the same time the *cafés cantantes* were beginning to experience direct competition as well. Regular programs were being set up and more performances were being offered every night on the *tablaos* in bars, not to mention the numerous flamenco festivals coming into vogue.

The tablaos were responsible for much of the loss of cante's intrinsic value. Hired to entertain a mixed audience of cabales and neophytes, some of the cantaores refused to sing lyrics that might "shock" the public. Thus the tablaos turned flamenco into a kind of stage revue, in which sex appeal and the excitement of zapateado displays took preference over the more typical aspects of a performance.

Many Andalusian cities at about the same time established flamenco centers of one kind or another that have now gone down in history. In Cádiz there were "La Habanera," "Palacio de cristal," "Corona," "La Europa" and "Los Tres Reyes"; in Cordoba "La Bombilla" and "Los Califas" in the Barrio de Mesquita; in Granada "El Carteró," "El Polinario" and "La Ciega de la calle de la Cruz."

Cabales subsequently established peñas, clubs dedicated to the performance, study and historical documentation of flamenco. Thus, the Peña Flamenca Gaditana "Enrique de Mellizo" was founded in Cádiz in 1973.

The study of flamenco, begun by de Falla and Lorca, was spurred by the publication of several important studies: *Flamencologia* by Anselmo Gonzales Climent (1955); *Geographia del Cante jondo* by Domingo Manfredi (1955); *El Cante Andaluz* by J. M. Caballero Bonald et al (1956); Donn El Pohren's *The Art of Flamenco* (1962); *Mundo y Formas del Cante Flamenco* by Ricardo Molina and Antonio Mairena (1963), as well as other studies by Climent, Molina, Blas Vega, Quiñones, etc. (see the bibliography).

A record anthology issued in 1955 was the first extensive collection of cante flamenco to appear; it included songs by several masters of cante who were then still alive (see Appendix G: Discography). Flamenco societies and flamenco specialists in the meantime began to sponsor *concursos* and gypsy-Andalusian flamenco festivals, many of which are still being presented (see Appendix A).

It was only after 1958, after all these initiatives had already made significant advances in research and challenged others to follow suit, that scholarly investigation of flamenco really began to proliferate. Strangely enough, most of those involved were and are writers and journalists, rather than scholars.

The Catédra de Flamenco de Jerez opened in 1958 and held the first Curso Nacional de Cante Andaluz in 1961 in Cádiz. This was followed by the Semanas de Estudio Flamenco (Malaga, 1963), the Semana Nacional Universitaria de Flamenco (Seville, 1964) and the Centro de Estudios de Musica Andaluza y de Flamenco, UNESCO (Madrid, 1968). In 1972, the Museu del Arte Flamenco opened in Jerez (see Appendix C).

Flamenco research also explored the relationship between flamenco and Latin American music. During the 1920s Pepe el de la Matrona and other flamenco artists who travelled to Cuba to perform returned with a variant called the *rumba flamenca,* which became known in Spain as the *rumba gitana. Guajiras* and *puntos* from Cuba, *milongas* from the La Plata and *columbianas,* which are called *canciones columbianos* in Colombia and are related to the Cuban *habanera,* also found their way to Andalusia.

In the last century many gypsies emigrated, either voluntarily or through deportation, to Santiago de Chile, Montevideo and Buenos Aires. A. Gonzales Climent has published a fairly extensive list of flamenco artists who were born in Latin America but moved to Spain.

It is no secret that Iberian music, and in particular Andalusian music, has left its stamp throughout Latin America. But the role of gypsy-Andalusian flamenco in the development of Latin-American music, in whatever form, remains largely conjectural. The *fandango,* the *zarabande* and the *chacona,* music described by Cervantes as variants "from India," are always mentioned in support of this theory. However, based on my knowledge of Latin-American music, there is absolutely no basis for this theory. Latin-American music is basically the product of acculturation of the Indians or Afro-Latins and is a melding of courtly dances (like the minuet, contra dances, quadrilles, waltzes and polkas of the ruling classes) with Indian and African songs and dances. Iberian folk music is likewise the result of acculturation, but unlike the Indians and Africans, the Spanish settlers were landowners. It is impossible to imagine that the gypsies, a much smaller group of people occupying a comparatively low level in society, could have reversed the normal pattern of acculturation. In Latin America, European culture met with a variety of native Indian cultures that differed widely from the rain forests to the coastal regions. Music and dance of both the lower and upper classes during the colonial period were predominantly group activities, often ritualistic in nature. Gypsy-Andalusian flamenco (in its early 17th and 18th-century forms) was, on the other hand, an extremely solitary form of artistic expression, collectively experienced. So it is probable that Andalusian folklore, which indeed helped shape flamenco, offered, as traditionally performed in a group, the more usual pattern for a blend of music and dance structures.

A New Era?

With the growth of the mass media, flamenco has entered a new era. Only a few good flamenco films have been made including the award-winning *Los Tarantos* (starring Carmen Amaya, La Singla and Antonio Gades) and Edgar Neville's *Duende y misterio del Flamenco* (1964). But what is to be made of Saura's *Carmen* or *Blood Wedding?* No matter how well Antonio Gades and his troupe dance in these films, or how well crafted, they have little to do with true flamenco.

Flamenco as the art of cantaores, bailaores and tacaores, performed for a close circle of spectators in an intimate and integrated atmosphere, becomes questionable if, thanks to the availability of video and cassette recordings, it can be repeated at any time—and indeed anywhere and before any kind of an audience. The cantaor Cepero complained: "Aficionados who can really become one with the cantaor don't exist any more" (Climent, p. 159). There is no doubt that early recordings of cante preserved priceless documents for researchers and aficionados. And indeed tape recorders should not be banned simply because of the special, direct intimacy of flamenco. On the contrary, records and videos are already replacing direct contact for some flamenco artists, even with those who might be expected to be their personal mentors. Cabales and flamencologists shake their heads and lament "the loss of mystery." Yet the question remains: Do those who record, study and follow flamenco as insiders have the right to comment on new directions undertaken by the artists themselves? An analogous problem, the strong influence exerted by non-performers, has emerged in other cultural arenas as well.

The integration of flamenco and theater is only one of the ways young flamencos can adapt their art to the times. Jazz and rock are not simply modern musical forms, they are also reactions of specific generations to the times in which they live. There is nothing unthinkable about combining flamenco and pop music. The only real question is whether flamenco-rock, for example, is still authentic gypsy-Andalusian flamenco. Would essential characteristics be lost in such a combination? In this connection a related question is whether this kind of combination is not absolutely necessary to appeal to Andalusian youth—gypsies among them—in order to save flamenco from becoming a dying art. Thus "Los Chunguitos", a trio made up of three gypsies from the *Extremadura* near the Portuguese border, enjoyed sudden popularity throughout Spain with two flamenco-pop songs from the Carlos Saura film *Deprise, Deprise*. This form of flamenco is not only easier for the public to "swallow", but even to embrace!

Flamenco can contribute to pop music its special rhythmic and melodic characteristics. It would not be the first time that a folk idiom has made a contribution to the larger musical world. It does not warrant being labeled commercialized, watered-down flamenco, provided its authentic form endures. Pop music has frequently taken inspiration from flamenco music's structure. But truly innovative ideas have rarely emerged, as was recently the case with gitano-bailaor Candy Roman's "Canti Romanti".

Jazz has seen some collaborations between flamenco artists and jazz musicians like Albert Mangelsdorff. Olaf Hudtwalcker, an art dealer, jazz buff and flamenco aficionado, tells how Albert Mangelsdorff spontaneously hugged the dancer Caraestaca "because he had such a fantastic beat." In 1967, the Basque Pedro Itturalde and his quartet recorded a flamenco-jazz album with Paco de Lucia. Miles Davis and Gil Evans ("Sketches of Spain") and John Coltrane ("Olé") incorporated into their compositions the flamenco they knew from listening to de Falla and others. Paco de Lucia made several recordings with John McLaughlin and Al Di Meola, in which Paco's "straight" guitar playing (without embellishments) is an important component of the sound of the group.

After stagnating during the Franco regime, flamenco experienced a renaissance. Flamenco had not been popular with the officials of the regime due to its inherent literary freedom. However, the new Socialist government, whose leader was himself Andalusian, brought new alcaldes (mayors) into the local government structures in Andalusia, alcaldes who were much more favorably disposed toward flamenco than their forerunners. A number of new local flamenco festivals and competitions were organized, either with or without the support of cabales and peñas.

But lately a new wave of Anti-Gitanismo has reportedly again raised its head in Andalusia. If so it might prove beneficial for gypsy-Andalusian flamenco—even though discrimination in all its forms is to be condemned—for pressure creates counterpressure which could well lead to a revitalization of flamenco from within.

It can be argued that it is the gypsy flamencos themselves who for too long have made concessions to mass audiences. As long as there were only cantaores, tocaores and bailaores, the fate of gypsy-Andalusian flamenco was never threatened. Its very character permitted it to resist any attempt at commercialization. The fact that true cante has failed to excite anonymous mass audiences has also to a large extent protected it from political repression. Thus gypsy-Andalusian flamenco as an art form is unlikely to be destroyed by outside forces as long as those inside do not give external forces the chance.

HISTORY OF FLAMENCO

Marion Papenbrok

What Is Flamenco Anyway?

The many attempts to explain the origin of the word "flamenco" have often appeared to be a quest for the most bizarre derivation rather than a genuine effort to trace its etymology consistent with a given author's expertise. Ricardo Molina (1971, p. 19) lists some of these supposed root words, most of which are from the Arabic: *felag-mengu* (migrant farmers), *felaicum* or *felahmen ikum* (farmer), and *felagenkum* or *flahencou* (Moorish songs from the Alpujarra region).

In each of these tortured derivations, one essential fact has been completely overlooked: the word "flamenco," which originally only meant "Fleming" or "Flemish," only became synonymous with "gitano" at the end of the 18th century and denoted a Spanish Romany. This fact makes its derivation from the Arabic, 350 years after the conquest of Granada, hardly plausible. The shift in meaning can undoubtedly be traced to the argot of the 18th century, in which "flamenco" in its adjectival form meant "ostentatious, dashing" and had a slightly negative connotation. This usage probably goes back to the Flemish soldiers of Charles V, whose arrogant behavior expanded the use of the word "flamenco" from the merely regional to the general. By the time this term was applied to the gypsies, its derogatory nuance had been lost, so that Charles III, who ended the centuries-long persecution of the gypsies in 1782, could safely propose "flamenco" as a substitute for the unpopular word "gitano." (This meaning of "flamenco" endures even today, by the way, reflecting a certain attitude toward life that is very difficult to translate: pride, self-confidence, style. It is also used to describe unusually courageous bullfighters.)

In keeping with this derivation, "musica flamenca" then simply meant gypsy music—in defiance of all those who refuse to concede that flamenco music originated with the gypsies. Only after 1782, when the persecution of the gypsies was ended, did this music begin to expand beyond its traditional place in the gypsy family circle, where it had always been inaccessible to outsiders. Up until at least 1860, gypsies were its exclusive interpreters; only after that date did the "payos," nongypsies, gradually start to learn it from them.

35

Today the musical definition of flamenco is not as clear as it was 200 years ago. In fact, almost every writer on flamenco tries his hand at a new, often highly individualistic definition of the concept and classification of the musical form, akin to the tortured way in which the word had been dealt with linguistically.

Cante jondo (Andalusian pronunciation of "hondo", which means deep or deeply felt), being the purest, originally tragic form, is often contrasted with a flamenco that is supposedly superficial (González Climent, p. 158) or too academic (Caba, p. 7) and used as a competing term. J. Carlos de la Luna tried to further divide flamenco into cante grande and cante chico. But these classifications all suffer from being highly subjective and of very little general applicability—the criteria for a definition being, so it seems, arbitrary.

Molina (1971, p. 21ff.) in contrast, endeavored to trace the historical development of various forms of flamenco; by doing so he succeeded, in my opinion, in coming up with the best system for classifying all the *cantes* and *bailes* that we call flamenco.

Starting with *cante,* i.e. singing (*baile*—dancing—plays a less important role historically), he defines flamenco as *cante gitano-andaluz* and divides it into two main groups:

—*Cante gitano:* the musical forms developed by gypsies who immigrated in the 15th century, and
—*Cante andaluz* (*agitanado*): the Andalusian folk music common to the diverse Andulasian folk groups, and only picked up and adapted relatively late (around the 19th century) by the gypsies.

The toná, soleá, siguiriya, tango and bulería belong to the first group; the innumerable variations of the fandango and the cantiñas, such as the alegría, belong to the second. Molina also identifies a third group, which he calls *cantes folklóricos aflamencados.* These are folk songs and dances from Andalusia, other Spanish provinces and South America, which were only slightly influenced by flamenco and therefore cannot rightly be categorized as cante gitano-andaluz. The sevillanas, the farruca, the garrotin and the rumba from Cuba all belong to the latter group. The cantes and bailes that originated on the Sacromonte and that have long since been replaced by a commercialized pseudo-flamenco, fall into a special category. They are a special variant of Spanish gypsy folk music, heavily influenced by Arabic culture, probably most closely related to the *tangos gitanos,* and sometimes accompanied by a chorus and a type of belly dancing. They, too, cannot be considered true flamenco.

Molina is very clear about the major role played by the gypsies in the creation of flamenco: They were the "blacksmiths" who hammered out the original flamenco from the "metal" of Andalusian music—a unique amalgam not found in other Spanish provinces nor in other Romany cultures. The stubbornness with which the thesis still persists, mostly in Spain, that the gypsies were "only interpreters" rather than creators of flamenco, reveals the ambivalent mixture of envy and admiration, fear and disdain that has always been directed toward these people.

History of the Romanichals

Beginning in the 18th century, linguistic studies reflected greater and greater certainty that the geographic origin of the Romanies was India. Most of them probably came from the Punjab in northwestern India, emigrating from there ca. 800–900 A.D. However, since the extent of Indic words and usages in the numerous existing variants of the Romany language differs, it is probable that their ancestors came from various provinces and spoke various languages. Even today, it is extremely difficult to identify the exact region from which they came.

We encounter the same difficulties in answering the question of whether the ancestral Romanies came from the same caste, and if so, which one. Clébert (p. 125–6), thinks they were Untouchables, while Kochanowski maintains they were Rajputs, that is, members of the warrior caste (lecture at the 2nd Romany Festival in Chandigarh, 1983).

The former hypothesis is supported by the amazing similarity between the "traditional" work done by Romanies and the work described in the Book of Manu as unclean and therefore done by lower castes: Namely animal trading, palmistry, acrobatics, music and dance, animal training and metalworking.

The latter theory is supported by the generally accepted fact that they considered themselves "aristocrats," in light of their practice of introducing themselves with noble titles when they arrived in Europe, and by the remarkable patronage by the European nobility they at first enjoyed.

But to try to deduce the Romanies' way of life and social position in their homeland from the work and modes of behavior 500 years after leaving India is reaching for a point. Too many questions remain unanswered. Why did they leave India? Did they live as nomads there? Were the trades they commonly practice now brought with them or learned later based on circumstance and necessity? In any case, the variety of trades practiced by Romanies in various European regions (and even among different groups in the same region) is extensive and this process of diversification continues. Not without reason do the names of some Romany "tribes" derive from the trades they have practiced, work which also distinguished them from other groups: Kalderara (coppersmith), Ursari (bear trainer), Lovara (horse trader), etc. Just when and where this specialization began is hard to pinpoint; but these trades hardly support the notion that the Romanies were formerly pariahs.

Nor is their frequent assertion of aristocratic origins proof that they actually belonged to the nobility. It may have been only a survival technique: As "persons of status", the Romanies could have been trying to gain the trust and support of the nobility. This support was short-lived, however. The groundwork for conflict in Europe had been laid.

As they journeyed through Asia and the Near East, they lived enough like the native inhabitants to avoid any significant conflict; at least no reports of major conflicts have been recorded. But in Europe this peaceful relationship changed. Initially the Europeans either admired or pitied these pilgrims and noblemen, while rulers took advantage of their talents as weapons makers and soldiers. But once their services were no longer needed, this relationship deteriorated rapidly.

From then on, the Romanies were viewed at best as serious competition to native craftsmen and their guilds, and at worst as footloose riffraff uninterested in holding steady jobs and whose strange customs and pursuits (palmistry, fortune telling, healing, animal training, etc.) soon made them suspect as practitioners of witchcraft. Moreover, like many other groups laid low by war, hunger and plague, they were forced to steal in order to survive. To make matters worse, escaped criminals and monks or nuns who had left their orders sometimes posed as Romanies (and even joined their bands occasionally), none of which helped endear them to the populace. Persecution, expulsion, and forced assimilation were elements of a "gypsy policy" that was universal throughout Europe. Spain was no exception.

The Romanies seem to have been particularly drawn to Spain, especially southern Spain. The predominantly oriental culture of Andalusia and the greater tolerance of its people made it easier for the Romanies to integrate there than in other provinces.

It is still unclear whether the gypsies came to the Iberian Peninsula only from the north (their appearance in Barcelona was first recorded in 1447) or also from the south, over the Straits of Gibraltar. Given their long history of journeys—frequently punctuated by extended periods of settlement, for example in the Near East—it remains a mystery why they should have avoided, of all places, North Africa. Perhaps their passage through that part of the world was simply never recorded, as the Romanies could not easily be distinguished, by appearance or lifestyle, from the diverse, mostly nomadic native populations.

Even today gypsies in the northern and southern parts of Spain draw a clear line of distinction between themselves. Moreover, there are a few Kalderaras living in northern Spain whom the gypsies call *Húngaros* and who belong to a completely different group. Strangely enough these two groups are not rivals; they acknowledge each other as gypsies, yet no intermarriage occurs. These facts lead researchers to believe that the two groups evolved along different historical lines.

Yet their fate did not differ in Spain from that of Romanies living in other parts of Europe. Accepted at first, they were soon ostracized, persecuted and finally hunted down like wild animals. In the 16th century, they were forced into ghettos for gypsies called "gitanerías," where they were encouraged to "forget" their nomadic ways. (The galley or some equally appalling punishment awaited those who refused to remain in their ghettos). Less than 100 years later, the ghettos were broken up and the gypsies were supposed to live among the rest of the population, become farmers and give up their cultural traditions.

But they did not become farmers, nor would they allow their families to be separated and forced to live apart. Rather, they chose to live outside the law as vagrants. Thus for centuries they were thrown together, especially in Andalusia, with two other groups of persecuted peoples who had, since the "Reconquista" (completed when Granada, the last bastion of the Moors, was retaken), also been denied the right to maintain their cultural traditions: The Jews and the Spanish Moors.

Andalusia

There is hardly another part of Europe with such a checkered history as Andalusia—one through or in which so many different peoples have passed or settled. Phoenicians, Greeks, Romans, Visigoths and Moors stayed in and governed this region, so easily accessible from the land or the sea, via the Straits of Gibraltar. Its profound penetration by other cultures and the many violent changes in sovereignty, with concomitant changes in the dominant culture, have left their mark on this province. The rich musical and poetic heritage of Andalusia, so inseparable from an all-pervasive, tragic-anarchistic view of life, has played a major role in the development of flamenco.

Of all the musical elements which went into the make-up of Andalusian folk music, the music which the gypsies discovered when they immigrated, we will only mention those which are historically verifiable and which made an essential contribution to the development of Andalusian musical culture between the 8th and 15th centuries:

—The old Indian systems of music notation, which were introduced into Spain via Persia by the singer and poet Zyriab. During the reign of Abderrahman II, he established and maintained singing schools in Andalusia;

—Moorish singing and dancing, whose influence, foremost in Andalusia, was felt into the 17th century;

—Jewish synagogue songs, from the 9th to the 15th centuries;

—Mozarabic folk songs, of which the most important were the "jarchyas" and the "zamras" (or "zambras").

All these influences fell on the fertile ground of a populace that had always been passionately devoted to music and dance—even Juvenal writes of how taken he was by the guile of the women dancers in old Cádiz. Andalusians also seem to have a particular gift for poetry. Even today, the ease with which they create spontaneous poetic metaphors is as impressive as their talent for lyric expression, despite a lack of formal education.

However, the reality of Andalusian history has been far less poetic. Every new ruler brought not only music and poetry, but upheavals, new laws, and new social customs.

The rule of the Catholic kings was particularly disastrous. Their policies with respect to the Jews and Moors of compulsory conversion or expulsion coupled with raids and moral despotism, created an atmosphere of fear and uncertainty throughout the province.

Andalusia's economy also suffered disastrously. Agriculture and finance, which for centuries had been in the hands of Moslems and Jews, especially in the southern half of the peninsula, and which served as the basis for a flourishing cultural and economic life, were brought to ruin in short order by the unlearned Christian "conquistadores." The masses were reduced to poverty as the land was sold off to the highest bidder: Latifundia management, under which southern Spain still suffers, reduced the former peasants to day-laborers lacking virtually any legal status. In the 18th and 19th centuries, 4%–7% of the Andalusian population owned the land, while another 70% were absolutely destitute. The countryside was swept by famines, against which the landless masses possessed no defense. In his *Historia de las agitaciones campesinas,* Diaz del Moral describes the situation in some of the Andalusian villages around the middle of the 19th century: People died of starvation daily; women sold plaits of their hair to feed their children (Diaz del Moral, p. 63–4). These unhappy conditions were suffered by the approximately 40,000 gypsies, living primarily in the area around the wine-growing center of Jerez de la Frontera.

Nevertheless, the gypsies living in Andalusia were better off than those in other provinces. The harsh, repressive laws were less strictly interpreted in Andalusia than elsewhere and the protection of the nobility lasted somewhat longer. Nobleman were frequently godfathers to gypsy children, which explains the existence of certain family names like Vargas, Heredia or Reyes among the gypsies.

Gypsies and lower-class Andalusians, whose lifestyles and social status were similar, lived together in a spirit of relative harmony, while the wealthier upper classes "condescended" to the degraded gypsies—a

situation not confined just to Spain. Nor, because Andalusia long remained a feudal society, did a middle class emerge that would disdain the Romanies and consider them a threat. Beginning in the 16th century a large percentage of Andalusian gypsies began to live a settled life; "gitanerías" were founded in Seville, Jerez, Cádiz and Granada, not under pressure from the authorities, but through gypsy initiative. These communities lasted (albeit interrupted by spasmodic attempts to disband them and expel their inhabitants) until this century as exclusive gypsy districts.

This settling down, which, after Charles III's edict of 1782, enabled them to live humanely, soon became the norm throughout Spain and should dispel any notion of "innate gypsy nomadism." Whenever Romanies have had a free choice between roaming or settling, they have opted for the best solution, both economically and socially, which could include living for long periods in houses (rather than tents or caravans). They kept (and remain) on the move largely to avoid discrimination and because their trades depended on moving from place to place. Should such occupations no longer pay enough and should Romanies have the chance to live and work in some other way, a more sedentary life is both practical and probable. And indeed this is what happened in Spain after the laws that had prevented gypsies from holding certain jobs and limited the number of gypsies allowed to settle in the same town were lifted.

First References to Flamenco

It was more than 300 years after the Romanies migrated to Spain that the first written references to their music appeared. In 1774, in his *Cartas marruecas,* Cadalso makes mention of the *polo,* which he heard at a private gypsy party (Cadalso, p. 77ff). It was still difficult, even in Andalusia, for gypsies to move about freely, let alone attract attention to themselves by presenting musical performances. So such performances were kept strictly within the circle of the family and its guests.

But after the historic edict of 1782, gypsy music emerged from its hermetic isolation, after which both Spanish and foreign authors in ever increasing numbers described and commented on this hitherto unknown art. Many of the songs and dances first mentioned no longer mean anything to modern readers; apparently these forms have died out. And although we recognize the names of some other songs, it is hard to know just how they might have sounded. Comparing the styles known since recordings became available, not only are enormous regional differences apparent but also the extraordinary development of flamenco depending as it does so heavily on the character of the interpreter. For despite the strictness of flamenco forms, room for a great deal of variation remains available—in fact, the few cantes offering slight opportunity for improvisation, like the polo and the caña, are considered "antiquated," drab and wanting in any real promise for expression.

Flamenco is largely sung by men. Many cantes were laments. (The *playera,* frequently noted in early accounts and considered a forerunner of the *siguiriya,* serves as an example. The name comes from the word *planir,* meaning to lament.) Their lyrics told of persecution, suffering and death. *Tonás,* the oldest form of flamenco, were only sung, never accompanied; other cantes were sung with only minimal accompaniment, usually by a simple beating of time with the knuckles or a small stick. Rhythmic clapping (palmas) was an early common practice, but a guitar accompaniment was infrequent. Although the guitar gradually gained acceptance, it was not used as a solo flamenco instrument until the 20th century.

The light-hearted cantes festeros were danced from early times, and were the domain of women. It never occurred to anyone to dance to the more serious cantes, at least not in public.

Up to the mid-19th century, artists were either amateurs or semi-professionals, for they could not make their entire living from flamenco, but pursued other paying trades as well, such as blacksmith, merchant or toreador. They traveled between villages and towns, paid by wealthy families to perform at festivities, or singing and dancing—for food and lodging only—at remote estates on the occasion of religious holidays, special gatherings of family and friends, or for whatever occasions that came up. Earnings from such performances were obviously very uncertain and the artist was furthermore often at the mercy of his host's whim: An artist was often engaged on the spur of the moment, the host having little understanding or appreciation of the performance. These private parties remain a source of revenue for flamenco artists. Pepe el de la Matrona and Péricón de Cádiz, two well-known singers, have graphically described in their autobiographies the humiliations that an artist in need of money suffered and continues to suffer.

The "Golden Age" of Flamenco

Around 1860, the situation surrounding flamenco began to change dramatically. The "cafés cantantes" (or "cafés de cante") that had come into existence in the early 1840s, offering a combination of food and flamenco performances, began to catch on. They began to provide a new source of income for the artists and served to reenergize flamenco, giving it a new creative thrust. This period of tremendous creative vitality is justifiably called the "golden age" of flamenco.

The café del cante offered the artists regular contracts, a fixed salary and, rather than whimsical "señoritos," an interested and critical audience who held their work in high regard. This newfound prestige and position, together with their professional need to constantly measure themselves against each other, encouraged the creation of new cantes and distinctive individual styles. Singers like Enrique El Mellizo, Tomás Nitri, Merced La Serneta, and Loco Mateo or "El Gloria" began to make names for themselves. Local and personal variants of the siguiriya, soléa, bulería, and tango (from which the *tientos* came) were increasingly heard. The role of tonás was reduced in importance while that of dancing and guitar playing was advanced. The gypsies now began to make use of Andalusian folk songs, changing and enriching them in their characteristic fashion. So it was that *cante andaluz,* which largely defines various forms of the fandango and the *alegrías,* developed side by side with *cante gitano.*

Around 1860, non-gypsies, or payos, began to sing cante gitano. The most famous of these was Silverio Franconetti, who recast the harsh, exotic songs into something more acceptable to the audiences' ears. Thus began a trend toward commercialization which ultimately was to prove harmful for authentic flamenco. The first signs of commercialization began to appear in the cafés de cante; an attempt was made to fit the sound of flamenco to the tastes of the public, which by now had grown to include not only adherents of "cante jondo," but also those who wanted lighter musical fare. And since every singer was not a Franconetti or a Chacón (the latter was also greatly respected by the gypsies and given the honorary title of "Don"), the artistic quality of the cante began to slip.

However, it would be short-sighted to dismiss all the cafés cantantes as decadent due simply to these negative aspects, as Machado y Alvarez did in the introduction to his collection of *coplas* (Machado y Alvarez, p. 11). The changes mentioned earlier—improved social conditions for the artist, the creative boost given flamenco, the greater degree of recognition for a heretofore "private" art—would not have been possible were it not for the cafés de cantes. The prominence gained by women as singers and men as dancers can only be counted a plus as was the growing importance of the dance and musical accompaniment, so that gradually they were employed with even the more serious cantes.

Yet it also became quite clear that, no matter how much Andalusian and "gypsy" music had intersected with and influenced each other, a complete synthesis was impossible. Even today, gypsy and payo interpretations remain very distinct.

Most of the former stuck to their old cantes—the soléa, siguiriya, toná, tango, bulería—but became specialists, cultivating their own particular style with inimitable perfection and empathy. The payos, on the other hand, often were "universalists," able to sing in various styles but concentrating primarily on the cante andaluz and leaving some cantes completely to the gypsy artists. Bulerías, for example, are to this day rarely sung, let alone danced by payos.

A few cantes have only recently—in the last few decades— emerged from the intimacy of the gypsy family and its personal celebrations. The *alboréa,* the traditional wedding song extolling the bride's virginity, was, and continues to some extent to be, cloaked in an aura of sanctity. It is feared that the presence of uninvited guests will bring misfortune both to "outsiders" who hear it and to the gypsy who sings it.

As audiences in the cafés cantantes (which continued to flourish until 1915) grew more and more partial to cante andaluz and its variations, the gypsies as well as those payos who refused to compromise their standards, withdrew to the milieu which allowed them to perform in intimate settings: Private homes, taverns and rural inns ("ventas"). This sealed the fate of "public" flamenco; its decline could no longer be halted.

Decadence and Renaissance

With the best of intentions but disastrous consequences, Antonio Chacón had taken flamenco from the cafés de cantes, which had become too small for the growing audiences, and transplanted it to the theater stage. No worse forum could have been selected for such an intimate art conceived in terms of an attentive, participatory audience.

The atmosphere of the theater completed the transformation that for decades fashioned the inaccurate picture the majority of people have of flamenco: Fandangos, cheapened to the point of unrecognizability; rumbas, milongas, guajiras, etc. from South America; sentimental songs called "cuplé flamenco"; borrowings from the zarzuela; and sensational vocal tricks, theatrical affectations and florid lyrics. But of authentic flamenco little was to be heard.

As time passed, flamenco came to be despised as vulgar and mediocre. In 1922, a group of intellectuals around Federico García Lorca and Manuel de Falla attempted to restore flamenco to what they knew it to be: A respected folk art with a long history. Together they started the "Concurso de cante jondo" in Granada. Much was made of it in the press and intellectuals attended in droves.

Unfortunately the organizers made a serious error: They thought of flamenco as belonging to all the Andalusian people, and only performers "from the people"—i.e. amateurs—were invited to perform. This misreading of reality led them to overlook the fact that even at the height of flamenco's commercialization, some professional performers were still able to earn their living without having to make any artistic concessions. Among the latter were such brilliant singers as Pastora Pavon ("Niña de los peines"), Manuel Torre, Pepe el de la Matrona and many others. However, they were not among those invited to perform in large halls; their names were familiar only to those who knew and loved the real cante gitano-andaluz and preferred it to popular stage spectaculars.

The "Concurso" organizers' romantic notion that unknown amateurs would emerge from seclusion who had preserved the treasure of the old, pure flamenco, proved unrealistic. In reality, the more an artist was forced to measure himself against others, the more he was exposed to differing personal and regional styles, the greater his growth and creativity—and such opportunities were limited almost exclusively to professional singers, dancers and guitarists.

Consequently, the amateurs who took part in the competition were mediocre. Prizes in some cante categories could not be awarded because none of the candidates was qualified. Those who did receive prizes included Diego Bermúdez El Tenazas, a semiprofessional from Moron, and the youthful Manolo Caracol, who in his later career sang some of the most awful "cuplés" but who, according to Pericón de Cádiz (p. 258–259), was, when among friends, a great interpreter of pure cante jondo.

The outcome of the Concurso was at best disappointing. Lorca and de Falla (whose earlier fascination with Andalusian music quickly waned after the competition) had failed to offer a new understanding of flamenco to a large audience. Meanwhile, lengthy theatrical spectaculars called "opera flamenca" became the rage, boosting the singers like Pepe Marchena to enormous popularity.

Under the Franco dictatorship following the Civil War, the opportunities for artistic development fell to their nadir. Commercial flamenco, with its superficial gaiety, was encouraged by state cultural policies because the picture of "cheerful poor people" in Andalusia fit its ideological concepts so well. If the popular fandango was often sad and sentimental, no one objected as long as it lamented a faithless lover or dying mother. But any social criticism, as frequently heard in the lyrics of cantes mineros, was forbidden. This lamentable state of affairs continued until around 1950, at which time a strange renaissance began to develop, coming as it did from outside Spain.

Theater and dance companies touring abroad and performing Spanish ballet and folk dances sometimes included flamenco troupes. These were usually of the more commercially-oriented kind, but now and then included some fine artists. Their impact was enormous. Audiences in France, Germany and North America began to suspect that behind the flashy facade, behind the shouting, the spangles and the flying skirts a music lay hidden that could express much more and whose origins were worth exploring.

Intellectuals interested in music visited Spain in an effort to trace the roots of pure cante jondo. On their heels came impresarios and record company representatives. Artists like Pepe el de la Matrona, who had enjoyed only an elite following in Spain, found himself singing to full houses in New York and Hamburg. The first flamenco anthology was recorded in France.

The Spaniards soon sat up and took notice again. An attempt in 1948 in Madrid to make the "old" flamenco available to a larger public— through the *tablao* "La Zambra," a new version of the café cantante—met

46

with an enthusiastic response and was widely imitated (Pohren, p. 81). Once again, good flamenco was being performed in such tablaos.

Yet in this new setting, and despite the high standards of the audience, the dangers of commercialization were unavoidable. Pohren (p. 82) attributes this vulgarization to the financial interests of the impresarios. But the singer Antonio Mairena, a gypsy from Seville who died recently, and to whom we are indebted for the classification and recordings of old cantes, felt the artists themselves were also responsible (Mairena, p. 174 ff.). In his view the ups and downs of flamenco had been injurious to its artists, so they failed to give the public credit for truly understanding and appreciating their art. This view led them to sacrifice authenticity right from the beginning. Mairena reproached many of the artists for their lack of integrity, sense of responsibility and courage. This, he said, posed the real threat to true flamenco. Mairena, for whom flamenco was the essence of the history and culture of his people and his homeland, warned against personal ambition and a single-minded focus on career, which would consume and destroy this immense cultural heritage. Those who have observed the events of the past few years are forced to conclude that his instincts were sound: The number of artists who mechanically grind out a fixed program at summer festivals and rake in their fees is legion. Their only thoughts seem centered on competition and stardom, a poisonous atmosphere for creativity. But fortunately there are countervailing trends.

New Directions

In the last few years the scope of flamenco has broadened considerably in three areas: Lyric repertoire, music and scenery. A large number of politically provocative lyrics have been added to the traditional repertory. Yet, in light of lyrics sung before the Civil War, this is not entirely new. Singers like José Menese and Diego Clavel have more or less specialized in these kinds of texts and have attracted large audiences, who find no conflict between such political statements and the historical roots of flamenco. Indeed, the intimate, personal laments sung in the past might easily be interpreted as veiled protests against deplorable social and political conditions, protests that could not be voiced explicitly. However, "political flamenco" is still rejected by many purists, and gypsies rarely sing it.

As a tribute to flamenco's Moorish roots, a few young artists like Lole y Manuel from Seville have interpolated Arabic elements into their music. Such innovations have proved to be highly complimentary to some cantes, particularly the tangos. This trend is especially popular among young gypsies.

Experiments with instruments other than the guitar have rarely been successful, as most instruments tend to distort the tonal quality of flamenco. The piano seems to be somewhat compatible. The music played by Pepe Romero and Felipe Campunzano (as representatives of gypsies and payos in this movement) is based on flamenco but has intense local color.

There is yet another trend based on flamenco, but it incorporates so many rock or blues elements that it can hardly any longer be called flamenco. Among those who perform this type of music are a group calling itself "Gualberto" and a singer named Manzanitas, who also performs classical flamenco.

Perhaps the most intriguing development is the use of flamenco in modern dramas, usually those with a political theme. The plays by a group called "Cuadra de Sevilla," are typical of this kind of theater. Using a combination of singing, dancing and pantomime, they portray the plight of the Andalusian rural population ("quejio") or the exploited industrial workers ("herramientas").

But the most intense and at the same time artistically brilliant productions are still those of Granada-based dancer and choreographer Mario Maya. "Camelamos naquerar" (which means in Caló, "We want to speak") concerns itself with the unrelenting persecution of gypsies documented by reading the edicts and legal texts extending over a period of five centuries, commented and elaborated upon through cante and baile. First staged the year after Franco's death, the political impact of this play was not lost on the Spanish right wing: participating theaters became fair game for slander and bomb threats.

Given these new contributions and developments in flamenco, it is hard to believe in the recurring prophecy that flamenco as an art form is about to become extinct. Let Pepe el de la Matrona, an old cantaor who strongly believes in the future of flamenco, have the final word:

> Maybe it will all go downhill again, like it did before—but who knows? Maybe tomorrow something will come along that is just as good as what we once had, maybe even better!
>
> Besides, when people say that without torture and prisons flamenco will die, I say: They are wrong. Why? Because people will always have feelings, joy and sorrow. Names and buildings, whatever—all that can change, but everything else stays the same . . .
>
> Even feelings themselves can change, but there will always be feelings. As long as the world exists, this will always be so . . . (Pepe el de la Matrona, p. 228).

THE SPIRITUAL WORLD OF FLAMENCO

Marion Papenbrok

A careful listener at a flamenco performance—one that does not implicitly assume an ignorant and superficial audience—is struck by its extremely dramatic quality. The acting of the singers and dancers—their painfully distorted faces, even when singing melodies sounding light and cheerful, or their expression of a deep, almost religious gravity— may be disconcerting to Central European and American audiences. The gestures of the singers and movements of the dancers betokening an enormous inner tension, a struggle—intensified by unexpected breaks in the melody or movement—these can reach a soul-shattering intensity.

Even the voices do not seem to conform to our esthetic definition of a "good voice." They are rough, even hoarse, and many passages are not really sung, but almost wailed, so that it is occasionally impossible to understand the lyrics. Moreover, each performer behaves like an abso- lute soloist on the stage. Granted, a singer and guitarist work very closely together, and in some cases dancers as well, but as to any form of genuine group performance—such as a chorus or group of dancers or even a couple dancing—none is evident. The soloist dominates every- thing; he or she is often surrounded by a group that participates intensely (by their commentary, encouraging words, and clapping without ever really influencing the singer's or dancer's performance.

This kind of performance is far removed from the folk singing and dancing we are used to. A completely different set of esthetics is operat- ing here, one in which expressiveness has a higher value than the concept of "beauty" as we know it. How did this sense of drama, the pas- sion and tragedy of this art come about? How are we to explain the excesses related by so many who have participated in flamenco ses- sions, usually private "reuniones"—people who burst into tears, tear their clothes, want to throw themselves out a window? (Pericón de Cádiz, p. 255, 239.) What irresistible urge drove Enrique El Mellizo to stand at the wall of the municipal mental institution at night and sing? Or Gabriel El Macandé, who always refused to accept any money for his art and who ended up in that same mental institution, singing his heart out to strangers and visitors, his body wracked by poverty and illness? (Pericón de Cádiz, p. 235; Cobo, p. 60). What is this duende (demon), whose effects on him García Lorca described, without being able to speak about its nature and origin except in poetic metaphors? (García Lorca, p. 1067–1079.)

The answers lie in the history of flamenco. Just as Andalusian music and the musical tradition and creativity of the gypsies determined the development of flamenco forms, the spiritual world of flamenco is rooted in the experiences and feelings of the Andalusian and gypsy peoples.

The preceding chapter described Andalusia as a region whose people were for centuries subjected, by a succession of rulers, both Muslim and Christian, to arbitrary rule, culminating in the great trauma of the Inquisition. Those dissenters who were neither expelled, killed nor "converted" by the Inquisition, continued their cultural traditions underground, but in the constant fear of being exposed or betrayed. "La fiesta interrumpida es un asunto totalmente andaluz" ("A party cut short is a strictly Andalusian phenomenon" Cansinos, p. 50). Cansinos (p. 123) concludes that there is a deep-seated feeling of *desencanto político* (political disillusionment) at the heart of all Andalusian people. By this he means a bitterness resulting from continued submission which is so profound that even when such treatment was past history, a distrust of any form of rule—and indeed of their own right to happiness—endured. They were left with a deep skepticism and an almost superstitious fear of the joy and richness life has to offer.

García Lorca's plays reflect this same sense of the futility in the pursuit of individual happiness. The moral conventions or material interests, which always lie in the way, are so powerful that no man dare oppose them. His characters become accomplices to the very powers that oppress them by foregoing any expectation of their own happiness. The single exception is Adela in *The House of Bernarda Alba,* but she must ultimately pay for her deliberate outburst with her life.

Feeling that they have been cruelly treated by a fate that was indifferent even to questions of life and death, the Andalusians have adopted a posture of stoic resignation. Yet they actively participated in numerous, often sudden and terribly violent revolts. Cansinos, Díaz del Moral, Calero and the Caba brothers have all documented the frequency and terror of such uprisings.

These revolts were abetted by secret societies like the "Black Hand" or, on the other hand, by toying with the idea of a communistic, or even an anarchistic society. So contradictory are the attempts to deal with an omnipotent destiny. . . .

But what is the bullfight if not the ritualized battle between man and powers bent on subduing him and against which he locks himself in battle? Of course the bullfighter's victory is only symbolic, the repetitions of the ritual cannot put an end to an ultimate sense of futility, and toreadors are seldom killed. "España es el único país donde la muerte es el espectáculo nacional." "Spain is the only country where death is the national entertainment," wrote García Lorca (p. 1078). As with flamenco, duende is an element of the bullfight. Specific stances the toreador assumes and moves he makes are described as "flamenco"; indeed most of the leading gypsy flamenco artists come from the same families as the great matadors. And that is certainly no accident. The same sense of futility arising out of repeated failures to vanquish the powers-that-be, which nonetheless are challenged over and over again, pervades the spirit of both flamenco and the bullfight.

Coplas, verses from Andalusian folk lyrics that have been taken into the flamenco repertory, bear witness to this feeling of futility: All the reason and will which man can summon in seeking beauty, harmony, happiness and an understanding of this world, simply crumble into despair in the face of the cruel absurdity which surrounds him—be it the behavior of rulers or matters of love and hate, wealth and poverty, health and sickness, life and death.

This outlook is reflected in the following verses, selected from among many in the same vein:

Pensamiento—aonde me llevas
que no te pueo seguir?
No me metas en caminos
que yo no puea salir.

My thoughts—are you taking me
  somewhere
I cannot follow?
Don't lead me down paths
I can't find my way out of!

Tengo yo un pozo en mi csaa
y yo me muero de sed
porque la soga no alcanza.

Though I have a well in my house,
I am dying of thirst
Because the rope is not long enough.

Dónde están los hombres buenos
que los busco y no los hallo
unos están en presidio
y otros en contrabando.

Where are all the good men?
I look but cannot find them:
Some are in prison
And the rest out smuggling.

En el viaje de la vida
van los ricos a caballo
los caballeros a pata
y los pobres arrastrando.

On life's long journey
The wealthy go on horseback,
The gentlemen (*caballeros*) walk,
And the poor drag themselves along.

Es tu queré como er viento
y er mío como la piedra
que no tiene movimiento.

Your love is like the wind
And mine like a stone
That never moves.

Se lo peí yorando
a la Binge de er Carmen
que me quitara a mí la salud
se la dé a mi mare.

In tears I prayed
To the Virgin of Carmen
To take my health
And give it to my mother.

A l'audensia van dos pleitos	There are two cases before the court,
uno verdad y otro no	One true, the other not.
la verdad perdió er juisio	The truth lost out
qu'er dinero lo mandó.	Because money spoke.

Yo no tengo más remedio	There is nothing left to do
que agachá la cabesita	But bow my head
y desí que blanco es negro.	And say: black is white.

Such themes of resignation and fatalism run through many coplas. Comfort is sought in communing intensely with nature, in reliance on a few trusted human relationships (especially with one's mother) and pleasure in little everyday things:

A las yerbitas del campo	I pour out my sorrows
les cuento lo que me pasa	To the grass in the field
porque no encunetro en el mundo	For there is no one in the whole world
persona de mi confianza.	I can trust.

Maresita mía	Dearest mother,
en un laíto e mi corasón	I will keep you tucked away
te traigo metía.	Deep in my heart.

Vengo de mi meloná	Returning from my melon field
traigo melones reondas	I bring round melons
y sandías colorás.	And rich, red watermelons.

Tienes los dientes	Your teeth
como granitos	Are like little grains
de arroz con leche.	Of rice pudding.

Yet fatalism and introspection are not the only themes in flamenco, as some biased assessments of the Andalusian mind would have it. Numerous lyrics deal with the struggle against poverty, oppression and violent revolutions:

Señorito a caballo	Master on horseback
que no das los buenos días	Who doesn't say hello:
si el caballo tropezara	If your horse should stumble
otro gallo cantaría.	You'll sing a different tune.

Obrero, por qué trabajas	Worker, why do you labor
si pa tí no es el producto	If the fruits are not yours?
para el rico es la ventaja	The rich take home the profits
y para tu familia el luto.	And your family reaps the mourning.

La tierra pa el señorito	The land belongs to the master
p'al obrero las fatigas	Only hardship remains for the workers.
Cuándo pensará el obrero	When will it dawn on them
deshasé estas injustisias	To throw off these injustices
que ayudan los manijeros!	In which the foremen are accomplices!

The list could go on and on, for the few coplas quoted are only a sample of their subject matter and mood, which range from deep resignation to a call-to-arms, reflecting the proximity of extremes so characteristic of Andalusia. In this land that produced both mystic piety and political anarchy, folk lyrics celebrate both the "good bandit" and the "fallen woman." It is precisely the extreme juxtapositions in these two prototypes that reveal the Andalusian willingness to break the law and moral codes for a "good cause"—violated honor, unconditional love, or the quest for justice—which ennobles the guilty and sets them next to the saints in an almost Gnostic juxtaposition of extremes.

Julio Romero de Torres, a 19th-century painter from Córdoba and hardly known outside Spain, elaborated upon just such paradoxical themes: Whores and nuns, bullfighters and men who commit crimes of passion. One of his most powerful canvases combines all these motifs in an uneasy combination entitled "Cante jondo."

But before de Torres could use cante jondo as a title the gypsies had to give it birth, for the outlook on life so characteristic of Andalusia seemed to culminate in them.

What the gypsies had learned in their nomadic travels was akin to the existential sense the Andalusians derived from the vicissitudes of their history. The temporal nature of their existence, the futility of planning for the future, were part of the baggage the gypsies brought with them when they arrived in Andalusia. The gypsies had also suffered at the hands of their rulers—though never for long, for the cruel persecutions which often thinned their ranks also led them to move on. They had hardly settled in Spain before they again learned they were not free to pursue their traditional way of life and could only survive, like the Jews and Moors, underground and in constant fear of pogroms and expulsions. At the mercy of an uncertain destiny and rootless in a hostile world, the immigrants rarely knew where they would be the next day, which forced them to concentrate more deeply on the common experiences of life than their settled Andalusian brothers. Wherever the gypsies settled in significant numbers, they found themselves on the bottom rungs of Andalusian society, sharing the same misery and hunger, the same need to survive by thievery and smuggling, and facing the same cruel punishments of imprisonment and forced labor. The world was simply a battleground, heartless and oppressive. The only answer possible was a cry, an expression of anguish, desperation and protest—a cry that was the origin and essence of what was to become flamenco. In the old cantes gitanos, the cry at the beginning of the performance became part of the song itself, as in the siguiriyas. The cry even replaced words, the human voice being used as an instrument, communicating, but not verbally. The plaintive "ay" that introduces and structures so many cantes arose as an instinctive personal reaction to deprivation and suffering shared by those present. This cry is conversation without words and the listener's empathy is its counterpart. In its purest form flamenco is a dramatic collective event, based on centuries of individual but shared experiences. The interpreter's power in expressing his emotions draws his audience into a common experience. He builds upon but goes beyond his personal anguish to articulate what he and his audience have in common: "Inexplicablemente, dolores y gozos seculares se amontonan en su garganta" (Mysteriously he gathers within himself all the pain and joy of centuries), said F. Quinones (p. 70) of such an "inspired" artist. It can be a frightening experience for the uninitiated to witness these profound emotional changes taking place within seconds in young artists—such levels of pain and suffering cannot have been known in their own lives, but must surely be drawn from some deep pool of collective experiences and memories. When the intensity of expression goes beyond the limits of time and the personal experience of the artist, then one hears the word "duende" used with great reverence and awe. It is said to be an irresistible power which possesses an artist only at very special moments and which leads the participants in such a "reunión" to such a state of ecstasy that they are led to rip their clothing, seem indifferent to fatigue or hunger, and are given to unrestrained crying or even aggressive actions—Manuel Torre is reported to have been bitten on the cheek by one so carried away in his audience.

The term "tarab", which José Heredia (interview) defines as "communicación a nivel profundo, casi irracional, communicación casi física, producida por una situación paroxística" (Profound communication, almost irrational, almost physical, caused by a state akin to a seizure), is used to describe such performances. The adjective "almost" in this context seems wrong: Such communication *is* irrational and produces genuine physical responses—blood pressure, heartbeat and sensitivity to pain can and do change, and consciousness is not infrequently altered. Flamenco is an hypnotic art and its means and effect, achieving ecstasy, a gnostic process. The music and the emotional excitement (typically enhanced by the lateness of the hour and the liberal use of wine and spirits) release the participants in this collective drama from the unremitting stress of life: External stress due to persecution, threat of imprisonment, hunger; internal stress arising out of existential fears, unfulfilled hopes and dreams, superstitious fears involving magic and demons, and the despair associated with the effort to understand an incomprehensible destiny.

These conflicts between man and the physical and metaphysical powers that threaten or oppress him, and his efforts to oppose them or his ultimate sense of resignation, are expressed with exceptional vividness not only in music but also in dance, since such conflicts and emotions can be directly translated into positions and movements. Thus, for example, the traditional interpretation of sexual roles, as well as the controlled, somewhat taboo relationship between the sexes is expressed in the very different dance styles stipulated for men and for women. The women's dance is statuesque, strongly dependent upon hand and arm movements, while the men's style is earth-bound and rational, defined largely by movements of the feet. In the few examples in which a couple dance together, they rarely touch—blatantly erotic gestures are confined to the commercial variety of flamenco. Spontaneous dancing is also frowned upon, for it disregards the strict code of form governing all flamenco, whether song, dance or guitar playing.

Conflict and suffering, as dealt with in flamenco, must be sublimated and overcome; if performances are free or chaotic, this sense of fitness is lost. Thus the beat—*el compás*—is considered the fundamental element in all forms of flamenco. What does it matter if the guitar is a little out of tune, the singer hoarse or the dancer grotesquely overweight—as long as the beat, which undergirds the emotional message, is right, the performance will be correct and expressive.

In such a context, there is no room for a concept so ethereal and dainty as "art for art's sake." Flamenco is the essence of a history and a culture in which all the participants in a reunión share. Through such a collective experience this fact is reaffirmed. While flamenco grows out of the historic consciousness of a singular people it also deals with common human experiences and sentiments not linked to any specific culture. How can we otherwise explain the enormous emotional impact and fascination flamenco exerts upon those who have never before seen a performance and know nothing about it? Only an openness to these common existential realities will provide access to flamenco, because flamenco arises not out of an effort to create an esthetic image, but from an elemental need to understand and come to terms with life and to find one's place in the midst of chaos and cruelty: "El difícil equilibrio entre cuerpo, alma y espíritu" (the difficult balance between body, soul and spirit) (González Climent, p. 169).

This deep-rootedness and sense of purpose in the life of its creators and interpreters is shared by both flamenco and the blues. Like the black slaves in America, the Spanish gypsies sought a way to express their suffering, to make life bearable enough to survive. Both forms of music fit the definition used by R. Molina (1967, p. 42) to describe early flamenco: " . . . Grito elemental—en sus formas primitivas—de un pueblo sumido en la pobreza y la ignorancia para quien sólo existen las necesidades perentorias de la existencia primaria y los sentimientos instintivos" (In its primitive forms it is the elemental cry of a people mired in poverty and ignorance, for whom instinctive feelings and the bare necessities of life are all that matter).

Just how fierce and extreme these feelings are can be demonstrated in a few lyrics selected from the classic and still sung flamenco repertory.

Cuando me echaras de menos	Should you miss me,
el día que me eches de menos	On the day you miss me
te tienes que volver loca	You'll go crazy
y has de salir a buscarme	And look for me
como el caballo sin frenos.	Like a horse without reins.
Lo que has hecho conmigo	You can never make up for
tú no lo pagas ni hecho cuartos	What you've done to me
ni puesto por los caminos.	Even if you were drawn and quartered
	Or banished for life.
Entre la hostia y el cáliz	
a mi Dios se lod pedí	Between the sacred bread and wine
que t'ajoguen las duquelas	I prayed to my God that
como m'ajogan a mí.	You would choke on grief
	Just as it chokes me.

These examples represent only a few of the many themes utilized in flamenco, but they clearly indicate the positive response to common, elemental sentiments. This intensity cuts across all flamenco forms: Singing, dancing and instrumental playing. In the absence of such intensity, flamenco becomes only a tawdry spectacle or empty technique.

"El flamenco está en la espontaneidad terrible del que sabe dolerse del mundo por cuenta suya y tener, arrebolada, la tremenda vocación del grito" (Flamenco, in its awesome spontaneity, is in him who can suffer from the world and feel within him—like the dawning—an irresistible urge to cry out) (González Climent, p. 214).

CANTE FLAMENCO

Christof Jung

The mid-day heat shimmers above San Miguel, the gypsy quarter of Jerez. It is only the end of May, yet daily the thermometer rises well into the 90s. On the patio of an old blacksmith shop where he used to work, the gypsy cantaor Manuel Agujetas stands at the hearth cooking fish. He is tall, lean, somewhat raw boned looking—"muy gypsy"—a *gitano de cuatro cosao,* a gypsy through and through (literally "on all four sides"). With his dark complexion and weathered face, he could almost be taken for an Indian. His powerful smith's hands deftly maneuver the pan on the hearth. A few aficionados and friends arrive and they eat and talk, the wicker bottle of strong *vino de Jerez* making its endless rounds. This is the setting for the start of a juerga, which will last until late at night. Some of the aficionados strike up a fandango or a *cante chico* and improvisations go on from there. But Manuel holds back; only occasionally does his highly expressive, hoarse *voz afillá* ring out with a spectacular fandango grande or malagüena.

Then suddenly he starts to sing *por martinetes,* one martinete after the other. The veins in his neck extend as he sings the difficult parts. He moves toward a state of ecstacy, "descending deep into his song" (muy jondo); his reserves of strength seem inexhaustible. His song laments the misfortune of being born a gypsy, the age-old suffering of his people living in filth and misery. It is filled with sadness, possesses a prodigious power of expression, is pure and archaic. There are no tricks, no acrobatic flourishes, sobs or long drawn-out "aaays." No, his cry is short—but it sears like a red-hot branding iron.

Martinetes

Desgrasiao de aquel que vive y come pan de mano ajena. Siempre mirando a la cara, si la pone mala o buena.	Unfortunate, he who has to live By taking bread from another's hand, Who always has to check the face To see if it approves or disapproves.
Estoy viviendo en el mundo con la esperanza perdia, no es menester que me entierren porque estoy enterrao en via.	I am living in this world Devoid of hope; There is no need to bury me Because I am buried alive.

I have heard many great cantaores, but none who were able to sing three or four martinetes in a row. But Manuel has been singing them for hours—it is unbelievable! Nobody here will dare to sing again tonight after this unique performance.

I never again heard Manuel Agujetas sing more perfectly or with such great intensity as on that night. When I asked him why he had exhausted himself singing only martinetes, he replied laconically: "Hombre, me ha gustao cantar por martinetes" (I just felt like singing martinetes)—"Y si no siento hambre, no canto" (And if I don't feel hungry [= don't feel like it], I won't sing).

Like many cantaores, Manuel has problems with flamenco festivals and recording sessions; it is difficult for him to sing well under pressure. He chuckled as he told me about one recording session scheduled at a Madrid studio for 8:00 in the morning to sing for three or four hours while being recorded: "As if you could sing in the morning!" "Por eso, amigo, mis discos no valen ná—son discos de maña" (That's why my records are no good—they're morning records).

Amazingly, he has memorized literally hundreds of coplas, many of them traditional songs whose lyrics he has altered and rearranged himself. However, he usually sings cante gitano, particularly siguiriyas, tonás (martinetes, debla), soleares and tientos, which he performs in a wide range of styles. He sings the cante "cien años atras" (going back a hundred years)—flamenco songs as they were sung in the last century.

Only after cante flamenco abandoned its true audience for a broader public—first in the cafés cantantes in the 19th century, later in tablaos in tourist centers and most recently in endless tours around the world—did people no longer understand it. Cantaors soon realized their dilemma in singing for non-Spanish-speaking audiences; they relinquished center stage to the dance (baile) and the guitar (toque). Flamenco shows presenting little or no singing are the order of the day. But the fact is that the origin and history of Andalusian gypsy flamenco is essentially the history of the cante and cantaores. Neither guitarists nor dancers had any significant role in what at the time was the revolutionary development of flamenco. The cante was the key factor in shaping the various flamenco styles.

In authentic Andalusian gypsy flamenco, the cante is and always has been the centerpiece, with dance and guitar taking their direction from it. The cantaor controls what happens, for flamenco is first and foremost a communication of feelings and meaning through song and not an audio-visual entertainment. And as a corollary the cantaor has an extensive repertoire of songs at his fingertips, which serve as a framework for his personal presentation of meaning and form.

Periods/History

Up to the middle of the 19th century the history of cante flamenco was identical with that of Andalusian gypsy flamenco. Baile and toque were only introduced later. Some essential facts from the preceding chapter on the history of flamenco bear repeating:

—The archaic forms of cante originated in the 18th century, but its basic forms undoubtedly took shape earlier.

—The cante began among the gypsies and was for years heard only in southern Andalusia (Triana [Seville], Cádiz, Jerez, etc.).

—The origin of cante is unthinkable without the cultural exchanges between gypsy and Andalusian folk music.

About the end of the 18th century, when the history of flamenco really began, most Andalusians were poor and destitute. The region was plagued by famines; often there was no work, or if there was it paid only a pittance. Bands of beggars roamed the countryside looking for food, and conditions were generally miserable. An English traveler, Townsend, reported in 1787: "The huts and houses in the towns between Ecija and Seville look like ruins; the peasants go about half-naked; the villages are crawling with bands of beggars; not just day laborers but artisans too are going hungry, and even small landowners beg in the streets of Seville" (Quiñones, *El flamenco, Vida y muerte*). The gypsies found themselves in the same straits, for they were of the urban and rural lower classes. Out of this misery, they raised their voices in songs that told the story of their despair and suffering. Singing seemed to make life more bearable. Cante flamenco became both a way of life and their outlook on the world. In the beginning cante was "kept under lock and key", performed only within the confines of the gypsy family, where its various styles and coplas were handed down orally.

The song forms now largely classified as cante grande (jondo) were those which came from this early period of flamenco, the "primitive phase": forms including the caña, carcelera, tonás (martinete, debla), corríos, playeras (early form of siguiriyas), siguiriyas, polos and soleares. The Andalusian–style fandango had probably already merged with gypsy songs by this time. By the mid-19th century, cante gitano had made its way to other Andalusian provinces as well. A kind of dualism developed between cante gitano and Andalusian folk songs. Once the cafés cantantes were in operation, cante gitano opened up somewhat to cante andaluz and the first "aflamencados" songs appeared in Andalusian folk music.

The Andalusian gypsy cante repertory expanded markedly during

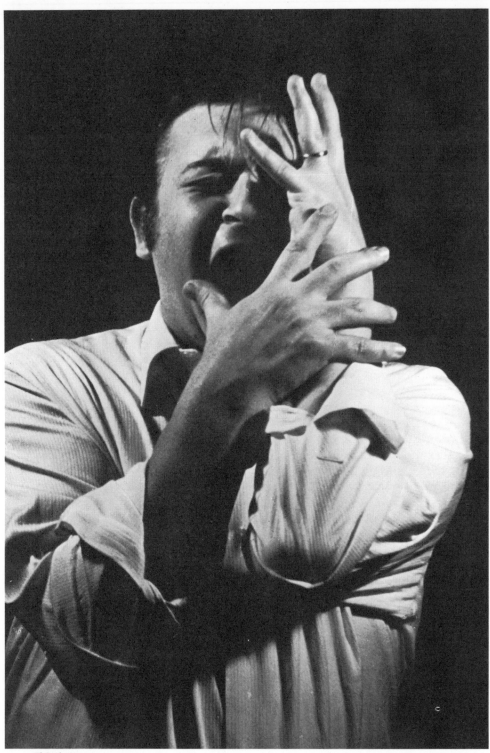

El Lebrijano

this period, primarily to those now called *cante chico* or light songs: Alegrías, bulerías, cantiñas, cartegeneras, granainas, romeras, tangos gitanos, etc. Meanwhile, traditional song styles were also evolving in gypsy circles.

This era has come to be called "La Edad de Oro" (The Golden Age). On the one hand, the cafés cantantes offered some improvement in the living standard for gypsy cantaores, who found in the café system not only better pay but a growing audience. But it was there that authentic flamenco also began to forfeit some of its purity. The cante lost its original function in the cafés: The solo expression of the collective feeling of a minority. *Cante para escuchar* (cante for listening only) was not in demand and so was replaced by a *cuadro flamenco*, which involved singers, dancers, guitar players and jaleadores grouped together for the first time. Performances in the cafés were increasingly dominated by professional musical groups who preferred the cante chico over the sounds of jondo which were considered to be monotonous and harsh. The former could be presented with a great deal more dancing, verve and showmanship than could cante jondo. Thus the idiom of cante chico was given a boost that would lead to its enormous expansion.

Despite such competition, authentic cante gitano owes to this period a large number of cantaores, who are still revered as creators of new cante forms and unsurpassed interpreters of traditional styles (Silverio, Tomás el Nitri, Curro Dulce, El Mellizo, Loco Mateo, La Serneta, Chacón, M. Torre, etc.).

"The 'Golden Age' of cante flamenco was followed, in the 1920s, by the age of 'opera flamenca'. This form of flamenco, with its lyrical falsettos and false, melodramatic cries . . . this poor excuse for flamenco, dolled up in flashy, academic finery to conceal its humble origins, now ascended the stage with all the trappings of the Spanish operetta (zarzuela)" (Manuel Urbano Pérez).

By 1910 many of the cafés were forced to shut their doors, as theater and opera companies took over chico flamenco. But this popularized version of flamenco was simply a travesty of what it once was. All that was left of its rich heritage were adulterations and couplets in a flamenco style. This unfortunate situation lasted until the early 1950s. Meanwhile, however, the gypsies once again proved to be the guardians of cante's authentic traditions, because they kept it "under lock and key." When systematic studies sparked a "rediscovery of flamenco" in the early 1950s, *flamencólogos* (flamenco specialists) were able to tap into the gypsies' vast underground resources. The singing styles of older, surviving cantaores, including of course some payos, were recorded for flamenco anthologies. The newly organized archives of the Cátedra de Flamencologia made an inventory of every sort of flamenco memorabilia that could be located. Books and countless recordings were issued to shed light on the history, diversity and meaning of flamenco.

Intellectuals suddenly took a burning interest in this music and for the first time a few non-Spaniards could be counted among the aficionados.

Elements of the Cante

Content

Most coplas (the texts of flamenco songs) are of anonymous origin; they simply arose from the great poetic well-springs of the Andalusian gypsies. Some have contended that the gypsies, the creators of flamenco, did not create the coplas used. However, the biographical content and descriptions of a unique way of life prove beyond any measure of doubt that most of the verses could only have been written by gypsy singers. This initial treasury of flamenco lyrics was later extended with coplas written by poets including Manuel Machado, García Lorca, Manuel Balmaseda and others. Like the structures of songs, coplas sung by the early cantaores were also passed down orally. Flamenco singers today still rely on traditional lyrics, enhancing them with their own variations.

In the often very moving coplas of the cante jondo, the singer communicates his personal suffering, using incidents from his own life; in only a few verses (usually of three or four lines each) he pours out a tragic story, the stirring lament of his own song becoming the song of human suffering. Sometimes with unadorned directness and sometimes with magnificent, lyrical imagery, the words describe the conflict between hope and despair, love and the pain of love, guilt and atonement, evil and divine protection. A sense of nihilism evokes a deep fatalism; death is one of the principal themes of cante jondo. *Mare* (mother), another common coplas theme, also knows pain (*Marecita de mi arma!*).

Penas tie mi mare	My mother sorrows
pensa tengo yo	And I too sorrow.
y las que siento son las e mi mare	But I feel my mother's sorrows
y las mias no.	And not my own.
	(Siguiriya)

Even the verses of the cante chico, despite their general joie-de-vivre, good humor and sarcasm, reveal a residue of sadness. They often give rise to impromptu poetry and, as in short chansons, contain well-aimed apercus with an amazing "precision of feeling" (Lorca).

Tienes los ojiyos grandes	What large eyes you have,
como pieras e molino,	As big as millstones,
y parten los corasones	And they grind up hearts
como graniyos e trigo.	Like so many grains of wheat.
Eres chiquita y bonita,	You are petite and pretty,
eres como yo te quiero,	Just the way I want you,
eres una campanita	Like a little bell
en las manos de un platero.	In the hands of a silversmith.
	(Cante chico coplas, type unspecified)

Although many cantes were born out of the worst sort of poverty and social injustice, their verses rarely contain any direct social criticism. Unlike songs created by other oppressed minorities, the words of the cante offer no solutions, nor do they contain any call to action to change the social and political conditions leading to such suffering. Indeed, coplas containing direct political statements were unknown in the 18th and 19th centuries. During the Franco regime, however, the political lyrics of two contemporary cantaores, Manuel Gerena and José Menese, were banned.

Verse forms

Coplas are made of verses of three, four or five lines. And while there are no hard and fast rules for the number of lines in the various song forms, alegrias, carceleras, tonás and martinetes usually have four lines; fandangos can have either four or five lines; soleares may have three. Nor are there set rules for ending rhymes in any of the cantes. Rhyme schemes like AABA, ABCB, AAAAB, ABCD, etc. are randomly combined. If several coplas are being sung (a siguiriya, for instance, consists of two, three or more verses), no logical connections between one verse and the next are required, so they often seem inconclusive and fragmentary.

Language

Most flamenco lyrics are sung in Andalusian dialect, Caló, the language of the gypsies, rarely being used anymore. Unlike other European Romany dialects, Caló became intermixed with the Andalusian dialect very early and has seen almost no use since the 19th century.

The few Caló words that have worked their way into flamenco coplas are readily understood and used by Andalusians generally. Perhaps there were still a few coplas in Caló at the beginning of the 19th century, such as the following:

Peno men ducas guiyabando	My sorrow I express in song
sos guiyabar sina orobar	For singing is crying,
Peno retejos quelarando	My joy I express in dance
sos quelarar sina guirrar.	For dancing is laughing.

But these coplas were put into Andalusian Spanish when the cante spread beyond its gypsy environs. Some of the Caló words that occasionally appear in cante are: *camelar* = love, want; *chanelar* = know; *endiñar* = give; *merar* = kill; *ducas* (*duquelas*) = pain; *eray* = Spaniard; *clisos* = eyes; *sacaiís* = eyes; *parné* = money; *garlochi* = heart; *undebel* = God; as well as the gypsies' names for themselves: *calorró, calé, caló.*

Musical Structures

The musical form of flamenco singing is not easily compared with that of other European forms, which makes it difficult for outsiders to understand. While the vocalizing techniques the cantaor uses are actually typical of those used in popular songs of many cultures, cante flamenco is unique in the way it combines these various techniques, combinations influenced by the many song styles the gypsies encountered during their travels.

The cantaor often uses half tones that are double-sharped, without leading to the next scale step (enharmonics). The interval spans a sixth. The cantaor needs this enharmonic "latitude" so that, in addition to the whole-tone scale, he has an abundance of tone colors to lend adequate shading to his emotional expression. This effect is heightened by repetitions, either of the same type or different, and by slurring or drawing out syllables and words (melismas).

The melody of the cante is often enriched by additional notes within the melodic line. But the cantaor uses these techniques "only when the emotional power of the words being sung suggests an expansion or sudden burst of feeling. Thus these embellishments are really more like expanded vocal modulations than ornamental passages" (de Falla).

The following melodic read-out of a siguiriya by Manuel Torre, as sung by his son Tomás Torre in the record anthology *Archivo del Cante Flamenco,* serves to elucidate the singing technique I am talking about:

Siempre por los rincones	I always see you
te encuentro llorando,	In the corners crying,
que libertad no tengo yo en mi via	May I have no more freedom in life
si te endiño mal pago,	If I am ungrateful to you.

Tiri ti ri ti..ay..ay..ay..ay..i..a..a..ay
ti..a..ay..i..
siempre por loo . . . siempre por loo..
rin..in..in..coné..o..ay
te e..en..encuentro..o..yorando
que libertá..aa..que libertá..aa
no tenga..a..yoo..o..en mi viivia..
si..i..si..i..te doy mar pago . . .
que no..i..tenga..a..la libertá yo..o..en mi viiaa..
si te..e . . . endiño . . . i..mar pago.

Thus the power of dramatic expression in cante jondo lies in the ability of the interpreter to project images vocally. The entire meaning of his performance stands or falls on his virtuosity, his intuition and his ability to convey to his audience the substance of the song and his personal emotions.

Even as early as the 19th century, many cantaores had made their favorite cante styles famous by virtue of their interpretations of them. A true cantaor never imitates! While singing, he is creating, an asset shared, incidentally, with contemporary jazz musicians, who also compose spontaneously.

A few early cantaores devised singing techniques so unique and powerful that they are still regarded as models, and "schools" evolved around them (Triana, Jerez, etc.). Thus we hear soleares in the Triana, Alcalá, Cádiz or Cordoba "style," as well as "according to" Loco Mateo, El Mellizo, La Serneta, Curro Frijones, Juaniqui, Joaquin el de la Paula, Tomás Pavón, etc. (See also section on the cantaores, p. 179).

The conventional European esthetic standards of a "cultivated voice" cannot be used to judge the vocal qualities of flamenco singing; only the cantaor's emotional expressiveness is important. Preferred vocal registers for cante jondo are:

Voz afillá (*voz rajo, eco gitano*) = deep, unpolished gypsy voice;

Voz redonda = sonorous, full, masculine, harmonic voice;

Voz naturá = natural voice, without any vocal tricks, similar to the *voz redonda*, only more expressive.

There are also the *voz facil* (soft voice) and the *voz de falsete* (melodic voice), which are largely confined to singing cante chico.

Structure of the Cante

The term cante does not simply refer to a song with various verses for it includes a number of components that build on one another and are organized according to classical rules of drama:

1. *Temple* (mood): Opening vocalization words; repeated "ay"s; tuning-up and getting into the rhythm.

2. *Planteo* (trial run): Introduction of and exposition of the melody.

3. *Tercio grande* (major third): Centerpiece of the song consisting of flamenco coplas, performed with all the cantaor's emotional intuition and power.

4. *Tercio de alivio* (relaxed third): The emotional intensity of the tercio grande is reduced.

5. *Tercio valiente* (forceful third): Here the cantaore forcefully projects himself and his personality, his style and inspiration.

6. *Cambio o remate* (change/conclusion): End or transition to the end of the cante. A similar cante is usually used during this transition.

Although often heard in theatrical flamenco today, a good cantaor never concludes a serious cante grande with a light, quick-paced cante chico, for by so doing he destroys the effect of his serious cante. But the reverse is quite common: Opening with a cante chico (or several) and proceeding to cante jondo.

Despite its seemingly rigid structure, the cante grande allows the singer enough latitude to vary the melody and formation of sound, especially in the tercio grande. But this latitude does not extend to a freedom to depart from the overall structure of the cante, which is determined for the most part by *compás* (rhythm).

Any deviation from these rules will immediately be noted and commented upon by aficionados.

Accompaniment to Cante

From the early days of flamenco until the middle of the 19th century, cantaores sang without accompaniment. They maintained the beat by tapping with a *palo* (style-stick). The guitar was recruited as an accompanying instrument, in addition to palmas, only after the spread of the cafés cantantes. The guitar expanded the tonal richness of the cante and relieved its monotony and austerity. Although the *tocaor* (guitarist) sets the rhythm of the cante, he only furnishes a musical framework for the singer. His playing marks the time, supports the song and keeps it on its defined course, for not uncommonly, in the heat of singing, a cantaor forgets what part of the cante he is singing. A virtuoso guitarist can break the singer's concentration, disrupting the normal course of the song, so a good tocaor limits his virtuoso display to ancient *falsetas* (melodic variations) in the song's introductory passages and in the intervals between tercios.

A cante pierces the silence. As the cantaor must muster all his powers of concentration to overcome the difficulty of the cante grande, only the calls of aficionados are allowed to break this silence, either to give the singer courage or to help him through a particularly difficult passage by encouraging and praising him (*Así se canta, eso es, muy valiente*).

66

Where the Cante Is Sung

Originally the cante was sung when pain and suffering became unbearable and the singer sought relief in song: In the fields, alone at night, while working at the forge or in the barn, on the patio of a tavern, or in the comforting environment of one's clan or family. The cante grande required a special ambiance and a particular audience. With only a few aficionados (cante admirers and experts) as listeners, it was possible to create the intensity of close communication. To witness the singer in his top form, all one had to do was wait patiently.

In the 1920s, after listening to Manuel Torre, (one of the most famous gypsy cantaores in the entire history of flamenco), Walter Starkie, the Irish authority on gypsies, wrote the following account:

> Many a time in Madrid or Seville the cantaor would be Manuel Torres, the greatest singer of Siguiriyas Gitanas, and one of the noblest Romanichals I have ever known. He was a tall, gaunt figure of a man with bronzed face and flashing eyes. His hair was jet black, but he had one white lock which gave a vampirish expression to his Oriental Wizard's face. He was capricious and moody and if there were a number of guests he would postpone his singing hour after hour. Don Alejandro would ply him with glass after glass of Manzanilla, Sevillian friends would allow him to boast that his greyhounds were the best in the world, still the great singer would sit motionless like a grim oracle, impervious to all our tricks. At last after hours of waiting, in the grey dawn, when we were thinking of leaving and when the other singers were exhausted, then Manuel Torres would begin tapping the rhythm with his short style-stick, and beads of perspiration would appear on his brow and his copper face would begin to glow as though suddenly illuminated by the inner demon, the *duende,* whose arrival he had been awaiting all the evening. Then he would burst into the great song (*Cante Grande*) which is "Deep Song," and we would listen enthralled to a *siguiriya gitana* expressing not mere natural suffering but a vague, everlasting pessimism—a tragic sense of life. (Walter Starkie, *A Musician's Journey Through Time and Space,* Geneva, 1958, p. 95f.)

Styles of Cante

Many attempts have been made to classify the various cante styles since flamencologists in Andalusia and Madrid actively began research on and documentation of cante. Each has been based on the researcher's estimate of how pure the cante was or how much Andalusian folk music was intermingled. Since the origin of most cantes is unknown, classifying them according to their roots is extremely difficult. They might as readily be classified by historical periods, i.e. when they first appeared, or according to literary criteria, and so on.

Molina and Mairena proposed the following classification:

1. *Cantes flamencos basicos,* the original gypsy cantes;

2. *Cantes flamencos,* related to or influenced by the above;

3. *Cantes flamencos* that evolved from the Andalusian fandango;

4. *Cantes folkloricos* (regional) influenced by flamenco.

Although this system seems reasonable, I find it difficult to use because the origins of most cantes are so obscure. I therefore suggest a traditional division into three groups, although I am also aware of the problems involved with this classification.

1. *Cante jondo* (deep song) or *cante grande* (important song)

Cante jondo is the essence of the art of flamenco and forms the foundation from which a multitude of other styles developed.

I know of no other body of folk song that has such dramatic intensity and tragic beauty. Pain, lover's grief, sorrow and pessimism are all conveyed in the poetry of its verses. Cante jondo is based on a complicated musical structure. Its melismas sometimes recall those of oriental songs. Almost all jondo songs are *cantes gitanos;* their best interpreters have been the gypsies, although a few payo cantaores have made names for themselves since the mid-19th century.

Examples: Cante jondo y grande:
Bulería por soleá, cabales, caña, carcelera, corríos, debla, liviana, martinete, playera, polo, pregones, saeta, serrana, siguiriya, soléa (soleares), toña.

2. *Cante intermedio* (usual song)

Although this hybrid stems from the cante jondo, it lacks the latter's seriousness (jondo), and usually has Andalusian roots.

Examples: Cante intermedio:
Granaina, jabera, malagueña, medio polo, mineras, petenera, policaña, taranta, taranto, tientos.

3. *Cante chico* (light song)

The structure of cante chico is not as complex as that of jondo; it is more melodic, more colorful and much easier to interpret. It also has deep roots in Andalusian folklore, as well as having assimilated musical forms from Latin American folk music.

Examples: Cante chico:

Alboréa, alegrías, bambera, bandola, boleras, bulería, calesera, campanilleros, cantiña, caracoles, cartagenera, chuflas, columbiana, fandango, fandanguillos, farruca, garrotín, guajíra, jaleo, lorqueña, mariana, media granaina, milonga, mirabrás, murciana, nanas, panadero, roás, rocieras, romeras, rondeña, rosás, rumba gitana, sevillianas, tangos gitanos, tanguillo, tiranas, trillera, verdiales, villancicos, vito, zambra, zorongo gitano.

What follows is a more detailed description of the most important cantes (with examples of coplas) from the above list of all known flamenco song forms:

Alegrías

(Cante chico with dancing and guitar accompaniment)

Cádiz, together with Jerez and Seville, was the center of cante jondo in the last century. As its residents were a cheerful people, a lighter style of flamenco also developed there called *cantiñas*. The most famous of these was the alegría, a festive song and dance.

Vente conmigo,	Come with me,
vente conmigo,	Come with me,
dile a tu mare	Tell your mother
que soy tu primo.	I'm your cousin.

Que el sentio me lo quitas	I can't think straight
cuando te veo en la calle	When I see you on the street.
que el sentio me lo quitas	I can't think straight,
y no paro de mirarte.	And I keep on looking at you.

Bulerías

(Cante chico y grande with dancing and guitar accompaniment)

We know very little about the origin of bulerías. At the end of the 19th century, Loco Mateo was said to be the first singer to conclude his soleares with a *remate* (ending) of bulerías. With its quick, spirited rhythm and mocking, often spontaneous coplas, the bulería is indeed the prototype of the *cante festero* (dance song). But originally this song was thought to have been quite serious. This gravity can still be heard in the *bulerías por soléa* (bulerías in the soleares style).

Bulerías can be divided into two groups:

Bulería al golpe = almost exclusively a song form (*cante para escuchar*);

Bulería ligada = accompaniment to faster-paced dance.

Es mi novio relojero	My betrothed is a watchmaker.
cada vez que viene a verme	Whenever he comes to see me
se la para el minutero.	The minute hand stops.

Toas son de carne	Everyone is made of flesh
mi compañera	Except my darling.
de azúcar cande.	She's made of sugar candy.

Bulería por soléa

Yo me quisiera morir	I would like to die
a ver si tú te ponías	Just to see if you would dress
negro lutito por mi.	In black for me.

Caña

(Cante grande with guitar accompaniment, rarely danced)

The caña, which probably comes from Cádiz, was one of the earliest forms of flamenco song. Writings on flamenco from the 18th century already make reference to it. It is a serious and very difficult jondo, sung by all the masters of cante. But it is rarely heard today. Many flamenco song forms, including the polo, soléa and serrana, derive directly or indirectly from the caña.

En el querer no hay venganza	Love knows no revenge
tú te has vengaito de mi,	Yet you took revenge on me.
castigo tarde o temprano	So sooner or later
del cielo te ha de venir,	Heaven will punish you.

Carcelera

(Cante grande, "a palo seco")

This pure cante jondo is one of the oldest forms of flamenco song and is the best avenue of expression possible for gypsy singers. Originating in the *cárceles* (prisons) of Andalusia, this tragic and expressive cante describes the singer's life and his loss of freedom. Because of its dramatic quality, it is extremely demanding physically. Today it is sung to the rhythm of the martinete.

Venticinco calabozos	The prison in Utrera
tiene la carse de Utrera.	Has twenty-five cells.
Veinticuatro he recorrio	I've done time in twenty-four
y el más oscuro me quea.	But the darkest yet awaits me.

Corríos

(Cante grande, "a palo seco")

Corríos are traditional romances and are among the oldest of flamenco song forms. The gypsies sang these in their own style, "a palo seco," i.e. with all the melismas and modulations of the cante jondo. Corríos were probably the basis for the tonás. Today this cante has been almost completely forgotten and is very rarely heard.

Debla
(Cante grande, "a palo seco")

Although we are still not completely sure of the etymology of the word "debla," it is assumed that this is the oldest form of cante jondo. The debla belongs to the tonás family of cantes. We know nothing about its original form, but the version reconstructed some decades ago by the great cantaor Tomás Pavón is now accepted as the model. Its extraordinary vocal demands put this tragic, almost sacred song beyond the reach of all but a few artists.

Yo ya no era quien era,	I am no longer who I was
ni quien yo fui ya seré;	Nor will I be again,
soy un árbol de tristeza	I am a tree of sadness
pegaito a la paré.	In the shadow of a wall.
En el barrio de Triana	In the barrio of Triana
se escuchaba en alta voz	One hears it loud and clear:
pena de la via tiene	If you are a gypsy
aquel que sea caló.	You must bear life's sorrows.

Fandango
(Cante chico with dancing and guitar accompaniment)

The fandango was danced in almost every region of Spain as an Andalusian folk dance since at least the 17th century. Its roots have been traced as far back as the Arab invasion. But the fandango forms used in flamenco are also thought to have been strongly influenced by the northern Spanish *jota* (a lively paired dance from Aragon). The fandango has numerous regional variations; the most widely known are from Alosno, Granada, Huelva and Lucena. There are two types of fandango, the *fandango grande* and the *fandanguillo*, the former almost as serious as the cante jondo, the latter being gayer and wittier.

A los racimos de uva	Your love is like
se parece tu querer	A bunch of grapes;
la frescura viene antes	First they refresh
la borraschera, despúes.	Then they intoxicate.
Mi caballo y mi mujer	My horse and my woman
se me murieron a un tiempo.	Died at the same time.
Mi mujer! Dios la perdone!	My woman, God forgive her!
Mi caballo es lo que siento.	But I really feel bad about my horse.
Porque no la conosia	When I didn't know about love
del amor yo me rei	I laughed at it.
y me enamoré de tí	Now that I'm in love with you
para que llegará el dia que	The day will come
se rieran de mi.	When they will laugh at me.

Granaina

(Cante intermedio, guitar accompaniment, no dance)

This *cante de levante* is still fairly new to flamenco and is a variant of the *Granada fandangos*. The melody is ornate, reflecting its Arab-Moorish heritage more strongly than other fandangos.

Gitaniya com yo	You will never find another
no la tienes que encontrar	Gypsy girl like me,
aunque gitana se vuelve	Even if all of Christendom
toita la cristiandad.	Were to become gypsies.

Liviana

(Cante grande with guitar accompaniment, rarely danced)

The *liviana* probably originated around the middle of the 19th century and was formerly sung without guitar accompaniment as a *toná liviana*. We now distinguish between two groups: *Cante campero* with its strong link to rural themes and folklore, and *liviana gitana* in which the influence of the toñas (debla, martinete) is more dominant.

Olvidé padre y madre	I forgot mother and father
por ir contigo	To go with you,
y ahora me dejas sola	And now you leave me all alone
por el camino.	Along the roadside.

Malagueña

(Cante intermedio, guitar accompaniment, no dance)

The malagueña came from the old *fandangos de Malaga* in the last century and became the quintessential flamenco song during the period of the cafés cantantes. Its musical structure has as many variations as that of the fandango. With its profusion of melodies and the beautiful elegiac quality of its coplas, the malagueña is surely one of the greatest flamenco song forms.

Cuando me pongo a pensar	When I stop and think
lo lejos que estoy de ti	How far away I am from you,
no me canso de llorar	My tears never cease,
porque sé que te perdi	Because I know I've lost you
para no verte jamás.	And will never see you again.
Mi llanto a nadie conmueve,	My tears move no one
cantando paso la via,	And so I sing my life away;
mi llanto a nadie conmueve,	My tears move no one
yo soy como el ave fria	So, like the little bird
que canta al pie de la nieve	Shivering at the snowline,
Al amanecer el dia.	I mark the break of day with a song.

Martinete

(Cante grande "a palo seco")

The martinete is the best known of the tonás. The gypsy smithies of Triana gave birth to this powerful song. Although originally unaccompanied, the martinete is now frequently sung to the improvised beat of a hammer striking iron. Interpreting this worksong takes enormous physical strength and is extremely difficult. There are two basic types: the *naturá* (natural) and the redoblao (doubled), the latter being the longer and more difficult.

Lo mismo que aplasto el jierro	Just as I work the iron
pa jacerlo filigrana,	Into a filigree,
quiero aplastá tu queré	I want to forge your love
de la noche a la mañana.	From morning to night.

Mara mia de mi alma!	Oh! My dearest mother!
Pare mio, qué verguenza!	Dear father, what a disgrace!
Que los gitanos se enteren	When the gypsies find out
que tengo la fragua en venta.	Our blacksmith shop is for sale.

Petenera

(Cante intermedio with guitar accompaniment, rarely danced)

The origins of this song are unknown and claims that it was influenced by Jewish synagogue songs have not been substantiated. The petenera is quite different from other flamenco songs, but its beautiful, measured rhythm reflects the influence of the soleáres.

Dónde vas, bella judia	Where are you going, pretty Jewess,
tan compuesta y a deshora?	All dressed up at this hour?
Voy en busca de Rebeco	I'm looking for Rebeco
que espera en la sinagoga.	Who's waiting in the synagogue.

Polo

(Cante grande with guitar accompaniment, sometimes danced)

The roots of this early 18th century song lie either in a popular folk song from the 1700s or in sacred music. It used to have many different forms, but only the *polo natural* is still being sung. It is closely related musically to the caña and the soléa, whose compás it adopted.

Toitos le piden a Dios	Everyone asks God
la salud y la libertad;	For freedom and good health,
y yo le pido la muerte	I, however, ask for death
y no me la quiere dar.	But this He will not grant me.

Saeta

(Cante grande, "a palo seco")

The saeta originally derives from the Holy Week liturgy, but its song structure in flamenco is influenced by the toná and the siguiriya. It was sung during Holy Week processions in Andalusian cities including Seville, Malaga and Granada. The singer intoned his saeta during pauses in the procession. His "ay" cut through the air like a saeta (arrow), sending his prayer-song soaring to the Virgin Mary and the crucified Christ.

Ya viene el Cristo moreno	Here comes the dark-skinned Christ,
el Señor de los gitanos	Lord of the gypsies,
el mas grande y el mas gueno.	The highest and holiest,
Apretaitas las manos	With hands bound,
Pobre Jesús Nazareno.	Poor Jesus of Nazareth.
Miralo por dónde viene	Look at the way He comes,
er Jesú de gran podé!	Jesus the all-powerful!
A cada paso que da	Lilies and carnations bloom
nace un lirio y un clavé.	Wherever he sets his foot.
Virgen de la Macarena	Virgin of Macarena,
reflejo de luna clara	The bright moon's reflection
da en tu carita morena.	Shines in your dark little face,
No hay cara como tu cara	There is no face like yours
ni pena como tu pena.	And no pain like your pain.

Serrana

(Cante grande with guitar accompaniment, rarely danced)

The serrana was probably a 19th-century folk song introduced into the flamenco repertory by the famous singer Silverio. By now it is a true flamenco song, heavily influenced by the rhythms of the caña, liviana and siguiriya. Its lengthy coplás tell of life in the mountains among bandits and smugglers.

Por la Sierra Morena	A gang roams
va una partia	The Sierra Morena
y el capitán se llama	And its leader is called
José Maria.	Jose Maria.
No será preso	No one will ever catch him
Mientras su jaca torda	As long as his dappled horse
tenga pescuezo.	Doesn't break his neck.
Al llover en la sierra	When spring rains fall
por primavera,	In the mountains
toman color de sangre	The streams turn
las torrenteras.	The color of blood.
Y entonces pienso:	And then I think:
Asi sera mi llanto	My tears will be like that
si caigo preso.	If I am taken prisoner.

Siguiriya

(Cante grande with guitar accompaniment, rarely danced)

It is almost certain that the siguiriya also derived from the toña. During the gypsies' long years of wandering—perhaps even while still in Persia—assimilated, foreign musical elements were incorporated into this song, as into all cante jondo. The first stylization of the siguiriya occurred in the playera at the end of the 18th century. The playera (the word is a phonetic distortion of *planidera*, lamentation) was one of the gypsies' simple burial and mourning songs. For aficionados, the siguiriya is the essence of flamenco. It is the saddest and most serious of all jondo songs. Boundless pessimism, unappeasable sorrow, the cruelty of fate, setbacks, death, the pain of love, mother—are all central themes of this lament. Due to its dramatic nuances, the rhythm of the siguiriya is indisputably the most difficult among the flamenco song forms and demands of its interpreter an enormous amount of emotional involvement. All the great cantaores have tried to master this song and to this day it remains the crowning glory of cante jondo.

No soy d'esta tierra,	I am not from this country,
ni en eya nasí:	Nor was I born here;
La fortuniya, roando, roando	Fate, rolling, rolling,
m'ha traío hasta aquí.	Brought me all this way.
Ar campito solo	I go alone into the fields,
me boy a yorá;	Go there to weep,
como tengo yena e penas	I seek solitude
el arma	Since my heart is so heavy
busco soléa.	With pain.
Las cosas del mundo	The things of this world,
yo na la jentiendo.	I just don't understand them,
La mitad de la gente llorando	Half the people cry,
y la otra riendo.	The other half are merry.
Horas de alegría	The happy times
son las que se van,	How fleeting they are,
que las penas se queden	While the sad times
y duran	Last
una eternidad.	An eternity.
Como sé que contigo	Since I know
no me voy a lograr	I can't get anywhere with you
así mis penas nunca van a menos	My torment will never diminish
siempre van a má.	But only get worse and worse.
Por esos munditos	In this world
me yaman er loco:	They call me the madman,
ar que tiene la curpa	But those to blame
e mis males	For my sad state,
yo bien lo conosco.	I know them well.

Pepe el de la Matrona (left), Pedro Soler (right)

Anhelaba vivir,
por verte y oírte; ahora que no te veo
ni te oigo,
prefiero morirme.

I longed to live
By seeing and hearing you;
And now that I don't see you
Or hear you
I only want to die.

Arbolito del campo
riega el rocio,
como yo riego las piedras
de tu calle
con llanto mio.

The little tree in the field
Is watered with dew,
Like the pavement
Of your street
Is watered by my tears.

Qué desgracia terelo
mare en el andar
como los pasos que
p'alante daba
se me van atrás.

What misfortune strikes me, mother,
Whenever I go about.
The steps
Meant to bear me forward
Carry me back.

Cuando yo me muera
mira que te encargo:
que con la jebra de tu
pelo negro
me amarres las manos.

When I finally die
Please do this for me:
Take a strand of your
Black hair
And bind my hands with it.

Soleares

(Cante grande with guitar accompaniment and dance)

We can assume that the current style of soleares arose in the Triana (Seville) barrio. Whether it was influenced by the caña and the polo is still debated, but what seems certain is that it evolved from the *cante para bailar* (dance song) and that it originated with the gypsies. The soleares, which is perhaps the most perfect flamenco song form, was, together with the siguiriya, the springboard for many types and variants of flamenco song. Its pathos and depth, coupled with what is probably the most beautiful compás in flamenco, make it one of the crowning achievements of the art of flamenco. The singer sings about pain of many kinds, while the highly poetic coplás contain fragments from the life of the gypsies and the people of Andalusia. The *soléa grande* consists of four lines while the *soléa corta* or *soleariya*, from which the bulerías derived, has three.

Si yo pudiera tirando *mis penas a los arroyuelos* *el aguita de los mares,* *iba a llegar hasta er cielo.*	If I poured all my anguish Into the streams, The waters in the sea would Rise to the heavens.
Los ojos de mi morena *se parecen a mis males;* *negros como mis fatigas,* *grandes como mis pesares.*	The eyes of my beloved Are like my troubles, Dark as my pain And big as my sorrows.
Hasta los árboles sienten *que se caigan las jojas* *y esta gitana no siente* *la perdición de su honra.*	Even the trees feel something When they shed their leaves, But this gypsy doesn't realize Her honor has been lost.
A mi mare de mi alma *lo que la camelo yo* *porque la tengo tan presente* *ay metia en il corazón.*	Mother, dear to my soul, How I love her, I will always carry her Deep in my heart.
Yo creia que el querer *era cosa de juguete* *y ahora veo que se pasan* *las fatigas de la muerte.*	I used to think Love was just a plaything, Now I see one goes through The agonies of death.
Unos ojos negros vi. *Desde entonces en el mundo* *Todo es negro para mi.*	I beheld black eyes. Since then everything in the world Is black for me.

Tangos gitanos

(Cante chico with guitar accompaniment and dance)

Despite assertions to the contrary, *tangos gitanos* were not influenced by the *tango argentino*. The former originated in Cádiz, Seville, Jérez and

Malaga and are also known as *tientos canasteros*. They belong to the more festive and resplendent group of flamenco songs and dances. Both the *tientos*, songs that are sad and serious, and the *tanguillos*, which are lighter and more exuberant, derive from tangos gitanos. Because they are gay and scintillating, tangos gitanos are among the main elements of flamenco and are masterfully interpreted by the gypsies.

Toitos los ojos negros	Tomorrow all black eyes
los van a prender mañana;	Are going to jail!
y tú, que negros los tienes,	Since you have black eyes too
échate un velo a la cara.	Hide them under a veil.
Que te quiero yo,	Oh, how I want you,
primita de mis sentrañas,	Dearest to my heart,
más que la mare que me parió.	More than the mother who gave me birth.

Tientos

(Cante intermedio with guitar accompaniment and dance)

Even though the old form of the tientos has vanished, we can still see that it evolved from the *tango gitano*. Its compás is slow and solemn and its musical structure borrows heavily from the soleares. The faster rhythm of the tango gitano is sometimes still used, but only at the end. The sad and majestic tientos number among the great flamenco songs and they, like the dance (which has all but disappeared), were forged from the experiences and spirit of the Andalusian gypsies.

Qué pájaro será aquél	What kind of bird is that,
que canta en la verde oliva?	Singing in the olive tree?
Corry y dile que se calle,	Go tell it to be still,
que su cante me lastima!	Its song makes me so sad!
Te vistes de colorado	You dress in red
y yo me visto de negro	While I dress in black
pensando que me has dejado.	Thinking you have left me.
Yo no sé porqué	I don't know why
esta gitana me vuelve la cara	This gypsy looks away
cuando me ve.	When she sees me.

Tonás

(Cante grande, "a palo seco")

This venerable flamenco song is also one of the earliest. At one time about 30 different variants of the toná were purportedly used, although only a few are now extant. Like both the debla and the martinete, tonás demand tremendous vocal technique. They are performed—without any fixed compás and without instrumental accompaniment—as a lament, full of sadness and pathos. As with so many other groups of songs, only a handful of lyrics still exist.

El dia paso con pena	The day is full of troubles,
y la noche con dolor,	And the night full of pain,
suspirando me anochece,	Twilight falls on my sighs
llorando me sale el sol.	And the sun rises on my tears.

Yo soy gerá en el vestir	Though I dress like a Spaniard
calorró de nascimiento	I'm a gypsy by birth.
yo no quiero ser gerá	I don't want to be a Spaniard
siendo calé estoy contendo.	For I'm happy as a gypsy.

The Cantaores

Beginnings and Golden Age

At the head of flamenco's 200-year history of song stands the name of the gypsy cantaore, Tío Luis el de la Juliana (ca. 1750–1830). He was a legendary singer from Jerez and noted for his tonás. One of the first great singers of cante jondo was a gypsy from Cádiz called El Planeta (ca. 1785–1860), who was instrumental in shaping the archaic style of cante and sang an extensive repertory of tonás, playeras, siguiriyas, cañas, and polos. "El Planeta's" siguiriya:

> A la luna le pio
> la del alto cielo
> como le pio que saque a mi pare
> de onde está preso.

> I implore the moon
> Up there in the sky,
> Implore it to help my father
> Escape from his prison cell.

Diego el Fillo (ca. 1800–1878), a gypsy from Puerto Real and a student of El Planeta, sang the first forms of siguiriya and cante "a palo seco." He is also credited with developing the siguiriya al cambio (cabales). The typical rasping vocal style of gypsy cantaores, called voz á-Fillá, is named after him. Silverio (1831–1893), whom García Lorca called the "last pope of cante jondo," continued to advance the course of cante flamenco. Silverio Franconetti from Seville, one of the few payos among the great cantaores, was also considered one of flamenco's most gifted singers. He was known primarily as a master of the various styles of siguiriya, including cañas and serranas. His great rival at the time was a gypsy from Jerez named Tomás el Nitri (ca. 1830–1890). He was a student and nephew of El Fillo, and we only know that his life was restless and eccentric. His singing, however, was one of the pinnacles of cante jondo in the 19th century. El Nitri created two difficult siguiriya styles and was the first cantaor to receive the "Llave de Oro del Cante" (Gold Key Award for Cante Flamenco), a trophy that until today has only been awarded three times. The legendary siguiriya interpreter, Maria Borrico (ca. 1810–1880), another gypsy, was one of the first female flamenco singers. Her contemporary, La Andonda, (ca. 1830–1890), also a gypsy, was the first, it is said, to sing the soleares. The gypsy Tio Rivas (19th century), an outstanding cantaor of corriás, tonás and cañas, originated the Cádiz style, together with gypsy cantaor Curro Dulce (19th century). Dulce was such a brilliant siguiriya singer that his style became a standard, and his siguiriyas, like his famous version of the caña, were widely imitated. Curro Dulce's caña:

A mi me pueden mandar   I can be ordered to serve
a servir a Dios y al rey,   God and my king,
pero dejar tu persona,   But no law can order me
no me lo manda la ley.   to leave you.

Cádiz, the white city by the sea, produced one of the greatest stylists in the history of flamenco song, the gypsy Enrique el Mellizo (1848–1906). Mellizo mastered all the various song forms and even created various styles of his own, such as the soleares de Cádiz, tientos and a type of malagueña with a slow, solemn compás. He was extremely influential and his style of singing had as many adherents as the style of soleares sung by Paquirri el Guanté, another gypsy son of Cádiz. Curro Puya, a gypsy from Triana, is remembered by aficionados as another important exponent of 19th-century cante gitano.

Triana, a district in Seville and home of the famous *gitanería* (gypsy quarter) "La Cava," was another place that played an important role in the development of flamenco. In the mid-19th century the gypsy clan known as Los Caganchos lived there. Gypsies from around the district would gather in the shed of "La Rufina," a little neighborhood store, for their famous juergas, from which all gachos (non-gypsies) were excluded. The Caganchos were blacksmiths and thus mostly sang *cantes fragueros* (blacksmith songs: Martinetes, deblas, carcerelas). The head of the family, Tio Antonio Cagancho, whose powerful voice made him an exceptional interpreter of the martinete, playera and siguiriya, developed the Triana style with his sons Manuel and Joaquín.

Manuel was to become the most famous cantaor in the Cagancho family. A few old aficionados, including the singer and writer Fernando el de Triana, remembered him:

A gypsy, old and downcast, with bronzed, almost blackened skin, he is a burly man, with huge, calloused paws, yet at the same time he is very dignified, likeable and modest. But then when he began to sing in his powerful, hoarse voice, all dark and clad in purple, with his dreadful and sudden *temple,* his voice growing stronger with every note, it made your hair stand on end. After such a performance it was not unusual for the enraptured gypsies to tear their clothes and smash anything they got their hands on, driven as they were to a kind of collective madness.

Manuel Cagancho was one of the greatest siguiriya singers in the history of cante gitano. But his version of the siguiriya, so full of melismas, is rarely sung any more because of its difficulty. Manuel Cagancho's siguiriya:

Reniego de mi sino	I renounce my fate,
como reniego de la horita, mare,	Just as I renounce the hour, mother,
en que la he conocío.	In which I came to know her.

Juan Pelao (1845–1910), a gypsy blacksmith who lived in the same barrio, is considered the greatest martinete singer of all times and an unparalleled interpreter of siguiriyas and soleares de Triana. But Frasco el Colorao was probably the first interpreter of Triana flamenco to become really well-known.

Jerez (de la Frontera), which produced so many preeminent flamenco artists, also had some great cantaores during this period: A true giant of cante gitano, Diego el Marruro (1850–1920) was a great singer of siguiriyas and martinetes: his siguiriyas are considered the most difficult in cante jondo. The siguiriya with "macho," a style invented by the gypsy singer Paco la Luz (1835–1900), is still popular. Another gypsy, Loco Mateo (1832–1890), was a professional singer specializing in the Jerez style and performed with his sister in the early cafés cantantes. His masterpiece was the soleá, to which he was the first to add bulerías. Another great gypsy master of the jondo during this period was Seño Manuel Molina (ca. 1820–1880), who was acclaimed for his powerful siguiriyas and martinetes, as well as his original tonás. Also active during this time was a gypsy singer from Jerez called La Serneta (1837–1910). She has been celebrated as the greatest soleares singer in the entire history of cante.

The great guitarist and siguiriya singer Juan el de Alonso, a gypsy from Jerez, was also influencing song styles during this period; Dolores la Parrala (1845–1915), a student of Silverio who had mastered all the forms of cante, was one of the best singers of her time; La Alondra (19th century), a gypsy from Puerto de Santa Maria, was also an important interpreter of soleares and siguiriyas. Three other gypsy interpreters from Jerez deserve mention here: the siguiriya singer Juanichí el Manijero, El Chato de Jerez (1850–1905), a student of Loco Mateo, and finally Tio José de Paula, who passed his singing style on to La Piriñaca.

El Puli, a gypsy from Jerez, was a famous cantaor of tonás, carceleras and martinetes. Seño Enrique Ortega, a gypsy from Cádiz known as "El Gordo" (Fats), was equally famous as a siguiriya singer and interpreter of cañas and polos. Another gypsy, Juanelo de Jerez, himself an unparalleled interpreter of tonás, was able to give Machado y Alvarez (Demofilo), the first flamencologist, invaluable information about various 19th-century flamenco artists and styles for his collection of *Cantes Flamencos*, published in 1881. Manuel Torre gained his fame from singing the difficult siguiriyas of his uncle Joaquín la Cherna. The gypsy Curro Frijones (1870–1930) was the greatest Jerez-style soleares cantaor, while El Carito (1835–1910) was a master of the Jerez cante gitano. Juan el Lebrijano (1847–1900), a gypsy from Lebrija, was a brilliant interpreter of cantes fragueros, mainly the debla and the redoblao, the most difficult type of martinete. Diego el Lebrijano's debla:

En el barrio de Triana	I want to write my mother,
ya no hay pluma ni tintero	Whom I have not seen for three years,
pa escribirle yo a mi mare	But in Triana
que hace tres años que no la veo.	There are no pens and no ink.

Juaniqui (1860–1920), another gypsy from Lebrija, worked his whole life in the fields of Andalusia and was instrumental in shaping the *soleares de Utrera*.

Juan Breva (1840–1915), a payo from Velez-Malaga, was another of the famous flamenco singers of his day. He was called "King of the Malagueña" because he sang it to such perfection.

Nineteenth-century cante flamenco, considered by many aficionados as its "Golden Age," came to a close with two gypsy interpreters from Alcalá de Guadaira (near Seville): Agustin Fernández, the father of Juan Talega, and his brother Joaquin el de la Paula (ca. 1847–1933). Together they created what was probably the most beautiful of all the soléa styles, the soleares de Alcalá. Joaquín el de la Paula's soleares de Alcalá:

Al infierno que te vayas	Whatever hell you choose,
me tengo ir contigo,	I have to go with you
porque yendo en tu companía	Because being with you
llevo la gloria conmigo.	Brings me such pleasure.

All of these cantaores, most of whom never performed professionally and usually only attained local fame, and others including El Bilili, El Rubichi, Antonio Farabú and Romerillo, gave the cante its final form in the 19th century. Cante has come down to us practically unchanged, especially the cante jondo.

Later Cantaores

The modern period of cante began with Antonio Chacón and Manuel Torre. Don Antonio Chacón (1865–1929), a payo cantaor from Jerez, was indisputably the most famous singer of his day. It was he who first popularized flamenco singing outside Andalusia through his frequent concert tours of the cafés cantantes. He was also responsible for creating several new song styles, including the *cartagenera,* the *media granaina,* and the *murcianas.* While many aficionados consider Chacón the finest singer in the history of flamenco, it must be recognized that his

Juan Varea (left), Pedro Soler (right)

enormous gifts were limited to the Andalusian cante chico. His lovely tenor voice simply did not possess the expressive power of the *voz gitano* needed to sing cante jondo. Manuel Torre (1878–1933), on the other hand, was the gypsy cantaor par excellence. Descendant of an old Jerez family, Manuel Soto Loreto, nicknamed "Torre" (The Tower) because he was so tall, began his singing career in his hometown. As a young man he made his way to Seville, which was then considered the Mecca for flamenco singers thanks to its many cafés cantantes. There he sang professionally and was well paid. Unfortunately his extravagant lifestyle and predilection for fighting cocks and English hounds ate away at his earnings and he died penniless in Seville. He was often reproached for his unevenness as a cantaor; he had neither the balance nor the confidence of other professional singers and was moody and eccentric. Yet on a good day he could sing the cante jondo so well that his audiences never forgot his performance. He sang the siguiriya (of which he knew many forms), to perfection, and must therefore go down in history as their finest interpreter. Manuel Torre's siguiriya:

Son tan grandes mis penas	So great are my torments
que no caben más,	I can no longer bear them.
yo muero loco, sin caló de nadie	Mad and with no one's warmth
en el hospitá.	I lie dying in the asylum.

The gypsy Juanito Mojama (1898–1958) made his siguiriyas seem like a dramatic prayer. In 1922, El Tenazas (1854–1929) took almost every prize for cante in the famous Concurso de Cante Jondo in Granada, arousing considerable attention with his interpretation of long-forgotten cantes. He was, in fact, the last great caña specialist. El Niño Gloria (1887–1937), a gypsy from Jerez, was the leading interpreter of the saeta. Another native of Jerez, José Cepero (1888–1960) had a lovely *voz redonda* in which he sang his marvelous fandangos. Gypsy singer Isabelita de Jerez (1898–1955) specialized in the old Jerez style. Though Pepe Torre (1887–1970), a gypsy from Jerez, was overshadowed by his famous brother Manuel, the few recordings he made show that he was an impressive siguiriya singer. The other winner of the "Llave de Oro del Cante" was Manuel Vallejo (1891–1960), a payo from Seville. Vallejo had a high voice like Chacón and was a gifted interpreter of the Andalusian style. One of the greatest interpreters in this century was a gypsy from Seville named Pastora Pavón (1890–1969). She was known as "La Niña de los Peines" because she began performing in the cafés as a child. She had mastered all styles of flamenco singing and her enormous repertory has been preserved in numerous recordings. Both Manuel de Falla and García Lorca were among her admirers. Her brother, Tomás Pavón (1893–1952), is ranked by aficionados today as one of the most brilliant cantaores in the history of flamenco. Pavón was a purist who sang only cante gitano and would have nothing to do with any of the Andalusian forms. He was a very reserved person who kept mostly to himself. Pavón almost never gave public performances, singing the dramatically beautiful cante jondo only for friends and admirers. His few recordings are regarded as a kind of sacred relic of cante jondo gitano. Tragically, his greatness was never recognized during his lifetime. When he was at the height of his powers (1925–1940), fandangos and pseudo-flamenco were so popular that authentic cante jondo could find no audience. He was responsible for resurrecting the debla, sang the tonás and martinetes of the Caganchos as well as various soleá styles, and was a siguiriya singer without equal.

Juan Talega (1890–1971) was a gypsy from Alcalá in the province of Seville. With his passing, one of the last great representatives of the old gitano style disappeared. His singing, noted for its unusual jondo, carried on the tradition of his predecessors El Marruro, Cagancho, Paco la Luz, etc. Manolito el de la Maria (1904–1966), also a member of Juan Talega's family, sang the incomparable soleares of his uncle Joaquin el de la Paula.

Pepe el de la Matrona (1887–) from Seville was a student of Chacón's and still vividly remembers the days of the cafés cantantes. Though a payo, this dean of the cante flamenco preserved the purity of the cante as few others had and passed on many forgotten styles. Pericon de Cádiz (1901–) and Aurelio Sellé (1887–), both from Cádiz, were the greatest interpreters of the Cádiz style in this century. With their gorgeous *voz flamencas* they intoned the soleares of Paquirri el Guanté, the malagueña and siguiriya of El Mellizo and, with their inimitable style and compás, the alegrías and cantinas of their native city. A few more names from the older generation should also be noted here: A gypsy named José el Negro (1906–) from Puerto de Santa Maria (near Cádiz), the last specialist in corríos; El Viejo Agujetas (1907–1977), a gypsy from Jerez and the heir to Manuel Torre's cante styles; another Jerez gypsy, El Borrico (1910–), a master interpreter of bulerías and cante grande; the unforgettable Tia Anica la Piriñaca (1898–), a recently discovered gypsy woman from Jerez with an encyclopedic knowledge of the old gypsy styles. Manolo Caracol (1910–1973) from Seville had a beautiful *voz afillá* and was one of the leading gypsy interpreters of the 20th century. Chacón found a worthy successor in Jacinto Almaden (1905–1968), and a gypsy singer Rafael Romero (1917–) sang cante jondo for years in the renowned flamenco tablao "La Zambra" in Madrid. Bernarda (1930–) and Fernanda de Utrera (1922–) are both compelling interpreters of cante gitano. Bernarda is still unrivaled as a singer of bulerías and the same applies to Fernanda for soleares. Our listing ends with Antonio Mairena (1909–1983), the "King of Cante Gitano." He was the third cantaor to receive the "Llave de Oro del Cante." It is due to him and others that cante gitano has regained its former place of honor. His extensive discography attests to his untiring efforts to maintain the purity of cante jondo.

The Younger Generation

Today young singers are trying to follow in the footsteps of their famous elders. While traditions are still maintained, today's world is different, even for cante flamenco, which means new forms of expression are being tried and experimented with. The following interpreters are only a few of the many new talents: Fosforito (1932–) is among the best flamenco singers in Spain. He is an outstanding singer of both cante grande and cante chico. Enrique Morente (1943–) from Granada is also one of the finest and most famous cantaores of the younger generation. He sang at "La Zambra" in Madrid and prefers to sing in Chacón's style.

The popularity of the young gypsy cantaores El Camarón (1951–) and Juan el Lebrijano (1940–) continues unabated and both have mastered large repertoires of cante jondo and cante festero. Also worth mentioning are three young cantaores from Puebla de Cazalla, a small village near Seville: Diego Clavel, master of the cante grande; Manuel Gerena, whose appearances were often banned during the Franco era because his copla lyrics were critical of the government and the social system; and José Menese (1942–), who is not a gypsy but sings in the cante gitano tradition. Menese is a sensitive interpreter of the various styles of cante jondo and one of the finest professionals currently performing.

I will wrap up this historical survey with three gypsy interpreters. First, Terremoto de Jerez (1934–1981), whose death meant the loss of one of cante gitano's most brilliant exponents. His *voz afillá* resounded with the jondo and duende of his ancestors and with the cantes de Jerez. The siguiriyas and soleares of this difficult school found their match in him. And his bulerías? Anyone who knows flamenco knows that there was never a greater interpreter of the bulerías de Jerez. Then there is El Chocolate (1932–) from Jerez, a cantaor with a highly expressive *voz gitana,* who sings all the cantes, but especially those from Triana. He has won countless prizes and awards, including the Premio Nacional de Cante. The singing of Manuel el Agujetas (1939–) revives the tradition of pure cante gitano in a unique way. El Agujetas began life as a blacksmith and became a professional singer only a few years ago. Flamenco experts were astonished by his first record because his cante style was so old-fashioned. Even the ancient masters of cante jondo had not sung any better and his song style had managed to capture this glorious past. He learned the old styles of cante, especially the cante of Manuel Torre, from his father. El Agujetas is, without exaggeration, the best cantaor of some song styles in Spain today. This is especially true of his exceptional interpretation of siguiriyas, several styles of which he has mastered: The cantes "a palo seco," tientos and soleares. He sings plainly and without much technique, but his articulation of the grief and tragedy in cante jondo is unparalleled.

BAILE FLAMENCO

Madeleine Claus

The Golden Age

The first notes of a siguiriya fill the room. A petite woman sits upright on a stool, her age clearly betrayed in her wrinkled face and dark, thinning hair. Her eyes are cast down, her arms held out from her body at an angle. She listens to the introductory "falsetas" and marks their rhythm with soft clapping. Concentrating intensely, she slowly rises. Her majestic bearing makes this small woman seem much taller than she is. She lowers her raised arms to her sides in a semicircle and then raises them to her breast, only to lift them in the air again. She holds her wrists loosely as her hands execute these circular motions. Although the dancer now opens her eyes, she seems to be looking through the audience into her own soul. With an elegant movement she tosses the train of her polkadot dress, stamps her foot once, twice and then gradually abandons herself to the deep intensity of the siguiriya. La Joselito is dancing. Flamenco. No gaudy, high-spirited spectacle accompanied by boisterous music, no sexy trappings. La Joselito's flamenco is different. Indeed, it seems more like some relic from the distant past. And yet it was not that long ago that this art form was taken over by show business and turned into the superficial tourist attraction it is today.

La Joselito was born at the beginning of this century, when the first professional flamenco artists were just reaching the peak of their careers. The quality of such performances was never again to be attained. Why? Probably because these people were the last to experience a time when Andalusians and gypsies, under the veil of oppression, sang, played and danced flamenco strictly among themselves, a time when concepts of life and death, love and work, routine tasks, fear and joy were only too well understood. These same artists were also taking their first steps up the exacting ladder of professionalism—exacting because audiences at that time were very knowledgeable and felt deeply about this art form; interest in flamenco was growing rapidly and audiences were willing to pay for it. This was the heydey of flamenco, the *Edad de Oro*, the Golden Age.

It was indeed fortunate that the technology of sound recording made its debut just in time to preserve some of that singing and guitar playing, thus giving us an idea of the exemplary quality of those performances. For the dance, on the other hand—intended for the eye as well as the ear—no such record exists. Yet just at this time, dancing was undergoing its most intense period of development. Even though written descriptions cannot adequately duplicate the true dimensions of this art, they might serve as a reference point—yet they too are absent. Indeed there would be nothing left from the heydey of baile flamenco were it not for a few isolated individuals like La Joselito who are still alive and were witnesses. People who see her dance, who talk with her, quickly realize that they have come face to face with the Great Era of flamenco. For not only did La Joselito live through the Edad de Oro, she helped create it. She has "forgotten" how old she is; age is without meaning when we are in her presence.

Her stories are replete with the names of the leading artists of this gypsy-Andalusian art, names that today are uttered with awe and reverence. They were all her friends, teachers and traveling companions: The singers Antonio Chacón, Melchior de Machena, and Pastora Pavón ("La Niña de los Peines"); the greatest guitarist Ramón Montoya; the dancers Juana Vargas ("La Macarrona"), Magdalena Seda ("La Malena"), Antonio de Bilbao, Juan Sanchez ("Estampio") and on and on. From the time she was six years old and was smuggled onto the stage, she performed regularly with these great masters.

La Joselito dances and sings flamenco. She *is* flamenco. She is a living encyclopedia, bearing witness to an art that survived for centuries only by being passed down from one person to another.

One has to be initiated into flamenco. For some time now, a few artists have been trying to develop new methods of playing the guitar and dancing, but without significant success. A student of flamenco needs a master. And with each master's death, a great storehouse of knowledge is gone forever. A copla on the death of the greatest soleá singer of the 19th century (she died in 1910) illustrates this flamenco way of thinking:

Cuando murío la Sarneta	When Sarneta died
la escuela quedó serrá	The school had to be closed,
porque se llevó la llave	For she took with her
del cante por Soleá.	The key to the "cante por soleá."

For me, this key to flamenco is La Joselito. Only such a person as she, who has lived in and with this art, can convey its meaning. And she is still alive, and she still dances. For without dancing there is no life for her.

La Joselito's relationship to flamenco is anything but intellectual: Dancing is in her guts, not in her head. Students who approach her to learn the techniques and spirit of flamenco do not get a dry lecture involving the latest teaching methods. On the contrary, the attitude of a

La Joselito

student in the presence of a "master" like La Joselito is probably more like that of the student of Zen.

Since my views have been influenced by La Joselito, they are anything but detached, or for that matter even objective. La Joselito's dancing moves me deeply. And I am of the sad conviction that nobody sings like La Niño de los Peines any more, that Ramón Montoya's guitar playing is still unmatched, and that the quality of today's baile flamenco is worlds apart from the dancing done at the beginning of this century.

This appraisal may not be fair to some newer trends, yet conversations with artists from the old days seem to support my partisan viewpoint. In the '50s, Ilse Meudtner was a dance student of Juan Sanchez Estampio, one of the last great flamenco dancers and at that time already advanced in age. She later wrote: "I learned that Spain was squandering an art form [nor has much changed since then—M. Claus.] It will still be carried on by a few people, but it won't be easy. Would-be artists are interfering, wheeling and dealing, ruining not only the profession, but the authenticity of flamenco's natural development—in singing, dancing and guitar playing—which, though world famous, is constantly under threat of destruction" (Meudtner, p. 75).

The recent trivialization of flamenco of which Ilse Meudtner complains has taken a huge toll on the dance. More than with singing or guitar playing, dancing has suffered under Spain's steadily growing tourist industry, which bills flamenco as its main attraction. For baile is surely the most easily understood element of this art that in the main strikes us as inscrutable and exotic, especially the singing. Through the dance, the excitement of this Andalusian gypsy art is transformed into a gorgeous image of physical movement—an image more readily comprehensible than learning to follow the unfamiliar sounds of the cante. In the end, however, this inaccessibility was a blessing in disguise. To avoid shocking the casual listener with this rasping, forbidding and introspective kind of singing, it was performed only as an accompaniment to dancing. The great flamenco singers sang only before small groups of aficionados or made recordings. This meant that their chances to perform were severely limited. By the same token, they were able to preserve their songs by not having to pander to the tastes of the public, which in its clamor for less challenging entertainment never suspected—and still does not—that the gaudy, high-spirited stage show has almost nothing to do with flamenco, but is simply a prostitution of this centuries-old art form.

Ironically enough, this transformation of the art of flamenco into show business began not with the onset of large-scale tourism but before that, at the turn of the century, during the Golden Age. The change from the almost familial setting of the private party to the demanding public of the cafés cantantes required performers to expand their repertoires and discover new forms of expression. The dance "spread open like a fan" (Grande, p. 362). Simultaneously a trend began to emerge that was to grow and spread as the years passed: Because the dance proved to be more commercially successful, increasing emphasis was placed on it in performances. Thus the balance that had always existed among the three elements of flamenco was now tipped in favor of the dance. It was not too many years later that both guitarists and singers literally took a back seat on the stage in order to make room for the dancers. By flamenco we now generally mean spirited heel-stamping to loud, so-called "gypsy" music.

Origins

Unlike the various styles of cante, very little research has been done on the dance, and what little has been written lacks adequate scholarly support. Nonetheless, the various trends in flamencology have tended to follow the same general lines. Andalusia has been the crossroads of several major Eastern and Western cultures as well as the destination point of the gypsies, who were also affected by great cultures. No one any longer disputes the fact that the cante jondo from this part of Spain was influenced by Persian, Byzantine, Greek, Hebrew and Arabic elements. Since song and dance have been interwoven from earliest times, these same influences have no doubt had their impact on baile flamenco as well. One commentator (Gobin, p. 61ff.) has traced a direct link to four major Indian cult dances (Katak, Kathakali, Manipuri and Bharata Natyam). Nor has this Indian influence on Andalusia been an isolated phenomenon, for in studying Andalusia's turbulent history, we repeatedly come across an Indian cultural presence.

The Indian past of the gypsies, Andalusian gypsies in particular, is posited chiefly on linguistic grounds. We can assume that their memories of this past were not completely extinguished during their extended wanderings through North Africa. But before the gypsies ever came to Andalusia, the influence of Indian music and dance could be seen, especially in Cádiz (then called "Grades"), the port city founded by the Phoenicians. Hindu dancers were regularly hired to entertain at large festivals (Gobin, p. 62ff.) and when the city was later occupied by the Romans, this tradition was continued. An epigram by the Latin poet Martial (born in Spain between 31–41 A.D., lived in Rome from 64–98) about a young dancer from Cádiz leads us to conclude that Andalusian dancing had already been exported to Rome. It is not certain exactly when and how Andalusian folk dance began to incorporate elements of Indian cult dancing, but at a very early date, Christians had already integrated some of these elements into their processions and religious events—despite their association with an alien religion.

Arabic influences can still easily be heard in cante jondo. In the case of the baile, the concentration on movements of the upper body—hands, arms and hips—as well as on footwork, probably goes back to Arabic sources as well, since the Koran, not to mention the moral code of the gypsies, forbade a woman to show her legs. But the dances of the Arabs, who occupied Andalusia from 711 A.D. on, had already been influenced by the gypsies who came through North Africa from India, that is to say, these dances, in all likelihood, already contained Indian elements.

But these are theories which, without thorough documentation, remain unconvincing. However, a closer examination of the shared elements of baile flamenco and traditional Indian cult dances demonstrates possible affinities—the distinctive play of the hands for example. And while gypsy-Andalusian dancing has no religious significance, baile jondo (the serious, introspective form of flamenco dancing), does possess something of a secular rite about it: Its god is Dionysos—the god who joins pain and pleasure in a state of intoxication.

Baile jondo

The almost "religious" intimacy of the artist and the profound seriousness of the baile jondo, which massive commercialization has increasingly degraded, are the very essence of flamenco dancing and express its basic soloistic nature. Today troupes of professionals dancing choreographed numbers are only too happy to pass their work off as "flamenco," but this is usually just "show biz" out for a dollar, with nothing authentic about it. Only a few forms of baile chico—lighthearted flamenco—are danced in groups: The sevillanas and various rural fandangos, which include the joyous verdiales. These group dances fall somewhere between true flamenco and Andalusian folk dancing, which, like gypsy folk dancing, had a great influence on flamenco (which is not folklore, but an art form!).

Pure flamenco dances were originally performed solo. This is the only format in which the real flamenco can emerge: the expression of an individual's innermost feelings and inner intensity. Only a soloist working within a defined format can give full range to his own improvisation, his own creation; only in this way can the "duende," that mysterious genius which sparks spontaneous inspiration in the world of flamenco, really take hold of the artist. Such individual expression is simply not possible when a *soleá* (a type of baile jondo), for example, is danced by four people following a closely choreographed, drill-like dance routine. Such a thing is only a mockery of the essence of flamenco.

This is not to say that group presentations cannot attain high standards of artistic quality defined in their own terms. Relatively stylized elements of flamenco have been successfully integrated into classical ballet, for example, and in so doing made a lasting contribution to this art form. Manuel de Falla's famous ballet *El Amor Brujo* ("Love, the Magician") is a good example of such a successful integration.

But the atmospheres of flamenco dancing and that of the classical Spanish ballet are worlds apart. Even the terminology makes this clear: A flamenco dancer is called a "bailaor," not a "bailarin" (ballet dancer).

The emotional power of flamenco comes from within the performer who abandons himself to his art, who breathes life into it. Flamenco is a profoundly intimate art, which is what differentiates baile flamenco from classical ballet. The movements of the two are exactly the opposite. Ballet takes to the air, seeks to be light, almost weightless in its movements and to hover by using spectacular gymnastics, while flamenco dancing is concentrated downward toward the ground, "the most intense energy right on the spot, tied to the earth, stamped into it" (Meudtner, p. 75). Psychic energy is transformed into physical, tellurian energy; catharsis is achieved in flamenco when body and earth are joined. The dancer seems to be dancing the theme of this connectedness, the theme of his own weight. The dance roots itself in the earth, as though drawn there by some powerful magnet. Gobin construes the all-important play of the arms in flamenco dancing, especially by the females, as a desperate attempt to lift themselves in the air as though on wings (Gobin, p. 112).

Classical ballet is an extroverted dance. Its choreography requires ample space, and even a solo dancer makes use of the entire stage. The introverted nature of flamenco dancing, on the other hand, is satisfied by an extremely limited space; an entire flamenco dance can be danced in a space no larger than a table top.

Two basically different sets of esthetics govern classical ballet and flamenco. Ballet dancers are youths in top condition with willowy, asexual physiques. Eroticism, on the other hand, is a basic element of flamenco. But this eroticism has nothing to do with the vulgar frivolity of tourist attractions that rely only on the sex appeal of their (usually young) female dancers. By contrast, some of the great flamenco dancers only earned their reputations when experience had given their art a certain depth and maturity. A flamenco dancer's career may only be beginning at the age when a ballet dancer is ready to hang up her shoes. Juana Vargas La Macarrona, queen of the bailaoras, was 60 years old and overweight when she reached her peak as a dancer. Until her death at over 90, she was the undisputed star of the tablao "Rosales" in Madrid. At the beginning of this century in Jerez de la Frontera, "an 80-year-old woman won a dance contest over beautiful women and girls with waists like candlesticks, and simply because she raised her arms, threw her head back and gave the stage a stamp with her heel" (Lorca, p. 114).

This art does not draw its power from outward appearances; it is not concerned with Beauty as we understand it. Flamenco does not care about an artist's sensitive soul, but about his guts. And when these are possessed by the duende—for this daemon has to be "roused" from the "innermost reaches of the blood" (Lorca, Beck, p. 60)—then something happens in the tablao, then all the power of flamenco is unleashed.

The Spanish poet Federico García Lorca, who was fascinated by flamenco, tried to explain this duende phenomenon in a lecture given in Cuba in 1930. He told a story about the singer Pastora Pavón ("La Niña de los Peines"), who had sung one evening for a select group of connoisseurs in a little taverne in Cádiz. "She played with her various voices, the one from the deep shadows, the one made of molten tin, the moss-covered voice; she entangled it in her hair, sprinkled it with manzanilla or lost it in the thick undergrowth. But all for naught." The audience was unmoved. The most important thing had not happened. Only when she sang "without voice, without breath, without any nuances, her throat scalding—but with duende," only then was she able to "shatter the whole structure of the song and let a savage, searing daemon emerge," and the audience "tore their clothing to shreds." " 'La Niña de los Peines' had to tear her voice apart because she knew that she was singing to an informed audience that demanded not the outward forms, but the essence—pure music with just barely enough substance to support it. Everything she knew and all the certainty she derived from it had to go; she had to send her muse packing and wait there, helpless and abandoned, for her daemon to appear and condescend to do battle with her. And then how she sang! Her voice no longer made music; it became a stream of blood, ennobled by pain and determination" (Lorca, Beck, p. 61ff.).

An art that turns its guts inside out and refuses to hide behind the mask of beauty—that is the real flamenco. Clearly this is not some superficial form of entertainment. Flamenco does not please, it is inherently not pleasing: "Neither the Spanish dance nor the bullfight are entertaining, not for anyone involved; the presence of the duende is the reason why the drama causes suffering" (Lorca, p. 118). Unadulterated baile jondo is much more closely related to the hoarse, strangely cracked voice of the singer than to the pleasant stage presentation glittering with virtuosity and technical skill. "The baile jondo is a spell, diabolical and dreadful" (Gobin, p. 111). In its remarkable synthesis of Apollonian beauty and Dionysian intoxication, flamenco is tragic in the true sense of Greek tragedy. But in flamenco, the Apollonian principles of strictness of form and tempered loftiness seem to have taken a back seat to the Dionysian element of pleasure: Insight into the suffering nature of all being induces a state of intoxication in which pain becomes pleasure. Only by respecting flamenco's soloistic character, borne on the tragedy and joy expressed by the individual artist, does this Dionysian art attain its cultural universality.

This quality forces immense demands on the individual artist. Some flamenco aficionados contend that only by making a pact with the duende can these demands be met. Does this mystic daemon only make pacts with those who have sold their bodies and souls to this art? Through their dancing, artists like La Joselito lead us to the essence of their lives as well as to the heart of flamenco and create in the audience some sense of the origins of this unique blend of oriental and occidental cultures.

Let us not fool ourselves—La Joselito has the body of a woman born into the world of flamenco at the start of this century. Spurning seductiveness, she bewitches her audiences not with her body, but by focusing their total attention on the art itself. Commercial productions, on the other hand, use "flamenco" to display the charms of frenzied, coquettish, plastic, imitation "Carmens." Alternatively, more ambitious productions of gypsy-Andalusian flamenco stress technique and virtuosity as ends in themselves. In either case, the ancient essence of flamenco is lost behind pomp and picturesque slickness, driving the duende into exile: Adieu Dionysus!—you've been banished by perfectionism and commercial interests.

Techniques of Baile Flamenco

The dazzling footwork used in flamenco dancing is often thought to be its most typical feature. But this view overlooks the fact that in the beginning the "zapateado"—a drumming sound made with the heel, toe and sole ("zapato") of the shoe—was performed only by male dancers. As it requires great physical strength, zapateado was long equated with manliness.

Females, on the other hand, danced the baile largely with their arms, hands and shoulders. Even though the distinction between male and female dancing is much less obvious today, more emphasis is still placed on upper body movements by the female baile. A slightly arched back is the classic bailaora stance, but is now often overly exaggerated. The arms are held in a smooth curve, unbroken by the bend of the elbows. "A woman's arms are supposed to execute undulating, caressing, almost sensual movements and her splayed fingers trace curling arabesques. The arm movements of male dancers are tighter, more restrained, even austere, portraying gestures that are highly geometric and descriptive: Arms cutting through the air like swords" (Puig, p. 223). Unlike the women dancers, men keep their hands closed.

In addition to zapateado, both male and female dancers employ "pitos" (finger snapping) and "palmas" (rhythmic hand clapping), often sounding at twice the rate of the beat. But the hands and fingers should not be used for anything else to leave them free for the important play of hands in the *baile de brazos* (arms). Castanets are therefore taboo—though they are widely considered typical flamenco props. Only classical Spanish dancing and traditional Andalusian group dances use castanets. Yet, because of their audience appeal, they are now *de rigeur* in every flamenco "show."

A truly authentic and important visual component of flamenco dancing is the *bata de cola*, the typical flamenco dress. Normally full-length, frequently made of a polka-dot material decorated with ruffles and flounces, it is clearly inspired by the colorful native dress of the gypsies. At about mid-thigh, the bata de cola flares out into a long flounced train, which was formerly starched, but is now simply backed with stiff interfacing. In what has become a classic element of the soleá, the siguiriya and the alegrías, the bailaora executes a series of elegant turns with this train.

The bata de cola figures in an anecdote told to La Joselito as a young girl about her famous teacher Juana Vargas La Macarrona. It was during a juerga in a café cantante, to which a wealthy *ganadero* (breeder of bulls) from Seville had invited all the greats of flamenco: Ramón Montoya, Antonio Chacón, Pastora Pavón, Manuel de Huelva, El Niño Gloria, Estampio, La Malena, etc. There he offered the young Macarrona 5,000 pesetas (the normal salary for a flamenco artist was 10 pesetas!) if she could dance in her bata de cola over 30 long-stemmed sherry glasses standing on a large tray on the floor without knocking any of them over. Juana gathered all her courage and began to dance in her pure white dress, whose train that day had fortunately been extra heavily starched. Not a single glass fell! With the money she was able to buy herself a place to live.

Male flamenco dancers usually wear dark trousers, a wide cummerbund and a white shirt with flared sleeves. Gypsies sometimes tie the shirt ends in the front. A short bolero vest called a *chaleco* is sometimes worn over the skirt. When women perform what were once typically male dances like the zapateado and the farruca, they too wear this costume.

Although guitar is now the instrument used to accompany dancing (and singing), flamenco was originally danced to songs. This was possible because older flamenco songs employ a strong beat. But to increase their expressiveness, singers began to place more and more emphasis on melisma, so characteristic of the flamenco song. This made many song forms, especially the fandangos and songs from the Levant, increasingly arrhythmic and less and less danceable, until finally they could no longer be danced to at all. Before the end of the 18th century, when the guitar became the accepted accompanying instrument, rhythm was kept with palmas, by striking bamboo sticks together, or by *nodillos* (rapping the knuckles on a table).

Perfect communication between the guitarist and the dancer must be established to create a successful dance performance. This means, by the way, that the music of the guitar is used as a backdrop—subordinated to the dancing and singing. The dancer does not dance to the music, the guitarist plays to the dance. Since the various dance styles have a definite structure—within which the artist follows his own inspiration and improvisation—guitarists have to be able to accompany a dancer without any previous rehearsal. Thus a guitarist has to be thoroughly familiar with the structure of a given dance and its basic steps; "saber su obligacón" (know your job), say the flamencos. The guitarist also has to pick up on the various conventional or spontaneous signs that orchestrate a dance: Steps—like the parade step, the "llamada," the "farruca" or the "desplantes," a certain sequence of steps that concludes a group of steps, reappearing like a leitmotiv—or certain movements and postures.

The alegría, known as the "queen of flamenco dances," is a typical female dance, although it has from its beginnings been danced by men as well (in which case more emphasis is put on the zapateado). The woman wears the typical bata de cola, with great importance attached to the play of arms and hands. Formerly the zapateado was rarely used and then only briefly. The alegría is an extremely colorful dance, whose parts are quite easy to distinguish. It thus lends itself to a more detailed description, which is no easy task (but a very "modern" one) when it comes to an art which affords such freedom to individual inspiration. Thus a flamenco dance is not taught in the sense that a structured folk dance or even a classical group dance is. A flamenco instructor never teaches his students an entire dance nor a complete choreography, but only its individual elements, which the student then fits together like a puzzle. Every dancer "builds" his own personal dance; even the course of an alegría depends mainly on what a dancer feels like expressing. So the following description only involves the traditional elements of a basic alegría.

The dance begins with a solo guitar introduction, occasionally accompanied by the palmero's *palmas claras* (loud hand clapping). Then the song begins. The bailaor stands on the stage and may also be clapping rhythmically; the bailaora is usually seated, also clapping and waiting her turn to dance. Even today, a man dances an alegría very differently than a woman. This is determined in part by the bata de cola, which calls for a special dance technique. The man opens with a vigorous zapateado, while the woman begins a series of choreographed steps with a short *llamada* (a parade step that is one of the steps alerting the guitarist to the structure of the dance to come), accompanied by artistic turns with the train of her dress. Both dancers conclude this first part of the dance with a *corte*. Like the llamada, which signals the beginning of a sequence, the corte is a step that signals the end of a sequence. Occasionally a zapateado is inserted here, but the next act of the alegría should properly be the "silencio" or the "rosas." This part is taken from the classical Spanish ballet, so the zapateado should definitely not be used, even by the male dancer. The dance now concentrates completely on the arms, hips, torso and legs. The mood is serious, controlled. The bailaora now has a chance to show how artistically and skillfully she can handle her bata de cola. She coils around the folds of her train, gathering them deeply on the floor, then to the muffled sound of her feet, she stretches her body up.

A short, quick llamada leads into the third part of the alegría, known as the "panaderos," "castellana" or "ida." Now the dance begins to approach the theme of its name *alegría* (joy). After the seriousness of the *rosas*, it becomes more playful, light-hearted, floating. The dance is still very much choreographed and the zapateado is rarely used. Its conclusion is signaled by a lively corte, usually followed by an impressive silence—the calm before the storm of the next act, the *escobilla*.

Now the zapateado takes over. This requires technical know-how and strength on the part of the dancer, as well as an ability to convey subtle nuances of sound. The length of the escobilla depends entirely on the endurance and skill of the dancer, who often concentrates totally on footwork without moving the rest of his or her body. The steps are symmetrical, that is, the left foot immediately repeats every step performed by the right.

Since the 1960s, it has become traditional for the dancer to break his dance off in the middle, the guitarist also stopping abruptly. Only the palmero continues to structure the sudden silence rhythmically with *palmas sordas* (muffled hand clapping). Then slowly, but with gradually increasing intensity, the dancer resumes his zapateado in a rhythmic dialogue with the palmero. The palmas only becomes *claras* (crisp) again when the guitarist resumes playing. La Joselito has a similarly impressive sequence in her zapateado: A spectacular solo done only with the heels (*el trino*).

The brilliant finale of the alegría bears the name of another flamenco dance, the bulería, whose frenetic mood, along with a few rhythmic shifts, is adopted here to create an entirely new dynamic. Both dances have identical rhythms (12 beats), but the bulería is much faster. After a brief llamada, sometimes performed with the dancer's back to the audience, and primed by the voice of the cantaor, the dancing, palmas and guitar assume a faster and faster rhythm until they all end abruptly at precisely the same time.

Styles of Baile

Although the repertory for baile flamenco appears to have expanded enormously in the last few years, this expansion has been misleading. For example, the famous flamenco dancer and bailarin Vicente Escudero, who died a few years ago, enriched the dance form by making the siguiriya, which had never been danced before, into a baile. But this cannot be said of present day dancers. They not uncommonly rename their creations in soleá style, calling them polo or caña. Caña and polo might be considered the grandparents of the cante por soleá. Form and mood of these songs are entirely different, although all three share the same compás (beat and rhythmic structure). For this reason authentic dancers like La Joselito contend there is only one dance, the soleá! I support this view of the classical, traditional repertory.

Several attempts have been made to systematize the various flamenco dance styles. José Udaeta classifies them in three different groups based on their rhythms. The first group, the soleá, alegrías and buleriás, are all dances in 3/4 time. Tientos, tango, tanguillo, zapateado and "by necessity" (Udaeta, p. 14) the farruca all belong to the group using 2/4 time. A third group, whose rhythm he leaves unspecified, includes the siguiriya and the peteneras (Udaeta, p. 13f.).

This system is probably less useful than the traditional two-fold division based on the cante forms: Baile grande or jondo, the heavy, serious flamenco dance; and baile chico, light, cheerful dancing. But some dances do not fit neatly into either grande or chico. A third category, *baile intermedio*, solves this problem. There are also individual styles that are sometimes grande and sometimes chico, all of which only proves how quickly any systematization of flamenco reaches the limits of its usefulness. If the categories grande or chico cannot be avoided, then the artists themselves should be categorized as chico or grande, for a jondo artist who is very jondo will dance a song classified in the lighter flamenco group and automatically make it deeper and more serious.

Because of these difficulties, I will not use such systems and will only refer to them where necessary. The *soleá* (baile grande), the "heart of flamenco dancing" and one of the most important in the dance repertoire, is a typical woman's dance, usually danced in the bata de cola. José Udaeta writes that Rosario Monje, nicknamed "Mejorana" and mother of the famous Pastora Imperio (singer of chansons influenced by flamenco called *canziones afflamencadas*), was the first to dance the soleá in the 19th century:

> She had a regal bearing and began her song by ornamenting it with lovely arm movements. These she accompanied with several slow steps around the small Sevillian stage, where she appeared nightly. Her performances were so successful that eventually she choreographed the entire song (Udaeta, p. 23).

According to La Joselito, this dance form reached its peak at the end of the 19th century, but disappeared in the 1930s for several decades.

The style of the siguiriya has been heavily influenced by gypsies (it is also called siguiriya gitana). But it was not danced until the mid-1920s, when Vicente Escudero "discovered choreographic possibilities in its rhythms" (Udaeta, p. 27 and 30). In 1946, Pilar López, primarily a classical dancer, was the first to use castanets with this dance. The siguiriya is now generally considered part of the basic repertory of flamenco dancing. Even La Joselito sometimes uses castanets with it "because the public likes it so well." But she admits that the siguiriya is more beautiful and more authentic when danced without castanets.

The alegría, "the queen of flamenco dances," is a typical female dance, though men have always danced it, placing more emphasis on the zapateado (see p. 97). This festive and at the same time regal dance was a specialty of the "queen of flamenco dancing," La Macarrona. Her alegrías only lasted a couple of minutes, but no one, according to La Joselito, danced them so incomparably. The bulería (baile chico)—the most popular flamenco dance at present—is often used like a sort of fireworks display at the end of a performance. Short solo numbers are accompanied by the clapping and coaxing (jaleo) of the entire cuadro, which provides amusing and acrobatic interludes, sometimes bordering on the clownish. The term "burlar" is the Spanish equivalent of "having fun." "All the reserve, the self-discipline, the majesty and line give way to a spontaneous outbreak of humor" (Udaeta, p. 23).

Much more serious is the farruca, whose prominent zapataedo immediately signals that it was originally a dance for men. It was "invented" in the 19th century by a dancer named Faico; at the beginning of this century it was stylized and expanded by Antonio de Bilbao. Ramirez, Manolito la Rosa, El Batato and Rafaela Valverde, not to mention La Tanguera, were all famous dancers who specialized in the farruca. Women have sometimes danced it wearing a pair of pants. (La Tanguera, for instance, was dancing the farruca in men's clothes at the beginning of this century.)

In the zapateado—also originally a man's dance—the bailaor concentrates on the contrapuntal drumming rhythm of his footwork while holding the rest of his body almost immobile. Females usually dance the zapateado in a type of outspokenly male outfit. This dance is often related to the Argentinian malambo, a rhythmic imitation of galloping horses, ascribed, not surprisingly, to the gauchos. The zapateado itself probably originated with Andalusia's mounted cowboys.

The song of the petenera tells of a woman who takes her revenge against men by leading them into misfortune, a kind of Spanish Lorelei. Gypsies never dance the petenera because they believe it brings bad luck. But the great singer La Niña de los Peines, a full-blooded gypsy, ignored this taboo by beginning all her performances with it. One day La Joselito asked her: "Why isn't the petenera danced?" "Oh, there's some silly flamenco superstition about bad luck," she answered. And so La Joselito, among others, created a choreography based on the song's hitherto undanced rhythm. It became one of Rosa Duran's most successful dances when she was performing at "La Zambra" in Madrid.

The garrotín is a typical light, cheerful flamenco dance (baile chico), to which La Joselito adds a slight coquettish twist. This is a relatively new dance style (19th century), whose compás is similar to a type of tango called a *tanguillo* (little tango). (The former is a baile chico that has nothing to do with the South American tango, while the latter is closer to Andalusian folk music.) The great Macarrona usually dances it as an encore, using a cordobés (hat) from the audience and incorporating it into her routine.

The taranto is a miner's song from the province of Almería, danced with a *passos saltados* (skipping step) that is more typical of folk dancing than flamenco. It was later interpreted and enlarged upon by various flamenco artists.

Finally there are the styles that came from Cuba, the rumbas and guajiras. These are extremely popular today and almost exclusively danced. Neither can properly be called a flamenco dance.

Rural group dances performed with castanets are only marginally related to flamenco. The above mentioned sevillanas are danced in foursomes of two partners each to four different musical numbers. At one time the fandango was danced throughout Spain, but it gained its real flamenco character in Huelva, thus its full name, *fandango de Huelva*. The verdiales, belonging to the family of fandangos, are popular group dances from Malaga. The rondeñas come from the city of Ronda, but are not the same as the rondeña which Ramón Montoya derived from the tarantas. The zambra is more correctly classified as a gypsy folk dance than true flamenco.

La Joselito

Flamenco is more than just music and dance: Flamenco is a way of life, a philosophy of life. It can only be learned by living with those who sing, play, dance and live flamenco. La Joselito grew up surrounded by flamenco and its inseparable sister art, the bull fight. Lorca defined the Spaniard's special relationship to death as the common metaphysical thread running through both flamenco and bullfighting, but there are other less mystical links between the two. The Andalusian pantheon is populated by flamencos and toreros alike. The names of Legartijo, Joselito, Belmonte or Cagancho are uttered with almost the same reverential air as that of flamenco maestros and maestras. Indeed the inexhaustible affiliations in love and life between these two ancient Andalusian worlds (the great torero Paquirri, killed in a bullfight in September 1984, was married to a flamenco singer) really remind one of the utterly human relationships between the Greek gods.

La Joselito bears the name of one of the greatest toreros of all times (he was killed as a young man in 1920 during a relatively minor corrida in Talavera), but her real name is Carmen Gomez and she is apparently a pure Andalusian, not a gypsy. She began dancing, by her account, when she was still in her mother's womb. She was only "taught" one dance, all the rest she simply "absorbed."

She speaks with great enthusiasm about the highs and lows of an historic period which she experienced intensely—as an artist, a woman and a human being. She is spellbinding even in a large group. Jumping up from her chair, this petite woman underscores her words with eloquent gestures and facial expressions; her youthful, blue-gray eyes twinkle and the gold bracelets on her wrist never stop jangling. She sits down again to sing a song, accompanying it with the familiar movements of her small, delicate hands. As she relates stories from her vast storehouse of memories, she often breaks into hearty laughter. Then she presses her left hand to her back, which gives her problems when the weather turns damp. But the moment she starts to dance her pain seems to disappear, for as long as she dances, time stands still and all the physical laws that try to bring her aging body down are repealed.

When asked about her past, Carmen Joselito, this little "grande dame," inevitably reminisces about her grandmother, La Berenguera, who was one of the towering female figures of classical Spanish dance and whose lifestyle was, for the times, rather atypical. At the age of five, La Berenguera was already dancing on the stage and she later toured all over the world. When she was 33—which in Spain was considered old— she became pregnant by a wealthy widower from Barcelona and bore the child out of wedlock. Nor was she married by the time she bore her third child, Elvira, who was to be Carmen's mother. After the former dancing star lost two men in quick succession, little Elvira supplemented the family's small pension by teaching a small dog to dance and incorporating it into her street act.

Carmen's father, Rodrigo Acensio, came from Almería in Andalusia. His parents died when he was still a child, so his older sister and her husband, who sold fabric and small metalwares from a caravan, took him with them on their journeys through Spain. When he was 15 he decided to fulfill his lifelong dream of becoming a torero. The mayor of a small village agreed to come up with a couple of cows so that Rodrigo, his friend Relampago and four other boys could practice bullfighting for the crowds in the village square.

The first cow caught Relampago on its horns and the boy only managed to save himself by rolling under an ox cart. But the cow—with Relampago's shoe dangling from its horn—wanted to get at him and had to be coaxed away.

Relampago was badly hurt—that's why we couldn't have children later on—and the mayor was furious. When my father saw all this he quickly gave up his dream and became a fishmonger in Barcelona instead.

It was there he met Elvira and her dancing dog. She was just fourteen when the two of them ran away from Barcelona. Her mother opposed their marriage and even Relampago warned that it was "much too early." "The woman I shall marry hasn't been born yet!" he told his friend Rodrigo. A few months later in Cartagena (Andalusia), where Rodrigo had found work as a miner, Elvira gave birth to Carmen. Her parents were finally married when she was 12 years old and seven of her 15 brothers and sisters had been born.

Carmen's memories are closely tied to the city of Barcelona. At that time—before and during the First World War—the capital of Catalan was very wealthy and supported a rich cultural life. When she was only eight months old, her father contracted black lung disease, leading her parents to leave Cartagena to return to Barcelona. It was there, when she was barely three years old, that Carmen began dancing in the market squares while her parents sold fabric from their newly purchased wagon. Two years later she went with them to Seville:

> There I first started "pilfering" dances. I took it all in and imitated it, giving it back in simplified form, of course. And pretty soon I could dance the sevillanas, the farruca and the garrotin. I learned the garrotin from La Coquinera. I sang it too. People were always amazed and enthusiastic. "Com'on Carmencita, dance the garrotin for us!" they would shout. I would don my father's hat, which came down over my ears, and start right in. Then they'd all slip me a couple of duros.

The family moved from one Andalusian city to another. She picked up the bulerías from the little girls in Cádiz. Her mother had given her a tiny dress with a train so when the day came that she met the greatest dancer of all times, Juana Vargas La Macarrona, she danced for her in the little bata de cola. La Macarrona was charmed. Later Carmen and her family journeyed throughout Spain, travelling as far as French Catalonia. Every year her mother had another baby, each time in a different city—the first nine being born in their caravan. When Carmen was six, her father's black lung disease worsened, so the family had to settle in Barcelona. And though her father took up fishmongering again, her parents found that they depended increasingly on the money Carmen brought in from dancing. "In the end there were 15 of us. Sick as he was, my father kept on making babies."

Shortly thereafter Carmen performed on the stage for the first time (this was still before World War I):

> Sometimes La Macarrona came to eat with us. One night she told my parents about a benefit to take place the next day, in which all the greatest flamenco artists would be taking part. I begged to go, but my father said I was too young. Macarrona gave me a wink and whispered: "Sneak out and get your little outfit with the sombrero and slip it to me quietly. I'll tell your parents you're coming to eat with me tomorrow!" She took my costume with her that night and the next day she came for me; I hid under the train of her dress. All the artists participating in this huge "cuandro" were seated on the stage. As the guitarist started to play the farruca for Ramirez, who was going to dance, I flew out from beneath Macarrona's skirts like a whirlwind, dressed in long pants and my little sombrero. Ramirez didn't know what hit him, after all, he was just about to start dancing! La Macarrona couldn't stop laughing, but the rest of them, especially Ramirez, were really furious!

Eventually Carmen became a regular dancer at the two largest cafés cantantes in Barcelona, the "Villa Rosa" on the Plaza Real, owned by the guitarist Miguel Burrull, and the "Casa d'Escanyo," named for its owner Joaquin Escanyo.

> Neither of them could stand one another. They fought over me like two butchers both selling the same piece of meat! One time my father even got into a fistfight with Burrull!

At these cafés, Carmen was always in the company of the greatest names in flamenco dancing: La Macarrona, La Malena, Antonio de Bilbao, Estampio, Ramirez and La Tanguera, to name but a few. The police were paid off so that she could perform at all. She would dance between 10 and 12 at night, so Carmen's father entrusted her to his old friend Relampago, who accompanied her on guitar in the cafés and walked her home right after midnight. It was during this period that she acquired her stage name:

> The great torero Joselito el Gallo often came to our shows and sometimes threw me a little money. He was courting La Coral's daughter, Consuelo Reyes, who could dance tangos and tanguillos so well. She was then 14 and often invited me to go to the movies with her in the afternoon. One night in the Villa Rosa, Joselito again tossed a couple of duros onto the stage to make me dance. Suddenly he raised his sherry glass, poured it over my head, and said, "I want you to take my name, because some day you're going to be very famous!" Consuelo, who was standing there, said to me, "Do you understand? From now on you're supposed to call yourself

Joselito!" Joselito himself was maybe 24 years old then. A couple of days later he and Consuelo eloped, using me as their alibi!

Rafaela Valverde or "La Tanguera" was another highly successful dancer. Like other dancers of that day, she performed only one dance, the farruca, but this she did extremely well. She seems to have been unattractive and large, her face covered with pockmarks. She was about 40 at the time and did not take well to the fact that little Carmen was upstaging her. During a performance one day at the "Circo Barcelonés" on the Calle Monserrat near the Ramblas, La Joselito received a particularly good round of applause:

The audience clapped like crazy. I was still so young and when you're young and you do something well, it really makes an impression. Tanguera had to dance after me and they hardly took any notice of her. She was a great farruca dancer but I couldn't help it if they liked me so well. When she had finished, she raced backstage in a blinding rage and wham! wham! she boxed my ears so hard they bled. I was practically deaf for three months after that. You could hear my screams through the whole theater. I threw myself on the floor and tackled her. She fell down, stood up and tried to hit me again. "You horrid little creature, I'll show you!" She was pulling my hair, when luckily a stagehand happened along and, seeing what was going on, grabbed me by the hand and ran out with me. On the way out we met my mother. Now here was a real Catalan! I can still see her with her apron on and a scarf over her shoulders. The stage-hand warned her, "You better watch out or that woman will beat your daughter again and again!" "What, beat *my* daughter?!" My mother happened to be carrying a garlic pestle in her apron pocket. She ran over to Tanguera, hauled out her pestle and began beating her with it. Tanguera defended herself, but even so she looked like a swollen turtle afterwards . . . But you have to hand it to her, she was a great farruca dancer. And I had danced her farruca! I copied it from her just like all my other dances.

Juana Vargas La Macarrona, on the other hand, took Carmen Joselito under her wing. The older woman was never jealous of the young dancer and was even able to talk sense to Carmen's partner, La Malena, who was a little touchier about Carmen's success. Carmen also got along well with the singer Pastora Pavón, "La Niña de los Peines." The other dancers were somewhat wary, but she continued to imitate their dances with astonishing ease. "Every step I saw went right into my coffer."

These constant squabbles and petty jealousies did not stop the flamenco artists of this great era from organizing a grassroots health insurance system for themselves. If an artist became ill, every performer chipped in part of his wages to cover doctors' bills and medicine. This system saved the 13-year-old Carmen when she contracted typhus.

With the proceeds from a special performance she was even able to spend four weeks recuperating at a rest home.

Several artists took to inviting her to travel with them to other cities in Spain. Ramón Montoya, the great guitarist, for example, took her with him to dance before King Alfonso XIII.

The money Carmen brought home had to be given to her mother on the sly, because her father was gambling away every penny he got his hands on.

A foreign woman who was obviously a great fan of Carmen's used to frequent her performances. She always threw money on the stage for her, which Carmen promptly folded together and tucked into her stocking.

> We called her "the Austrian." Sometimes she gave me so much money we could all live on it for a month. Well, once when I was 12, my mother took me to Paris, London and Belgium to appear in a show with the Argentine master of tango, Carlos Gardel. In the newspaper one morning we saw a picture of this same Austrian woman. My mother recognized her at once. That's how we found out that she was Mata Hari, a German spy who was later executed in Paris.

When she returned home from this tour, on which Relampago had, as usual, accompanied her on the guitar, Carmen's father discovered that his old friend was courting his daughter. He took this as a terrible breach of trust: "He was so angry he wanted to kill Relampago. And he wouldn't let him accompany me any more, no matter what."

She then worked with a number of other artists: Ramón Montoya, Juan Habichuela, Mariscal, Pepe de Badajoz, Perico el del Lunar and Miguelito Burrull. Together with a large cuadro of 40 performers, among them Antonio Chacón, La Niña de los Peines and other dancers, she made tours through Spain that included extended stays in Madrid. During this period she received the only dancing lesson in her life—to learn the zapateado.

> Antonio de Bilbao, who was by far the best dancer of the day, was a good friend of my father. He loved to eat fish and wash it down with a glass of something, even though his doctor had forbidden him to drink because of his heart. One day when I was in Barcelona, he was visiting my father and I said to him adoringly, "Maestro, when you die, no one will dance the zapateado any longer!" That was his specialty, you see. He looked at me and said, "*You* will dance the zapateado!" And he taught me how. I had learned all the other dances just by watching and imitating. He even showed me some steps from the men's alegría that I could dance without the bata de cola so everyone could see my feet.

Regla Ortega

Carmen was now a young woman of 18 and being courted by a famous torero, Valencio Primero. But when she returned to Barcelona after another trip, she ran away with Relampago:

I loved him. He hid me in a wardrobe in his mother's house. But my parents notified the police. (I was only 18 and in those days you were still considered a minor until you were 23.) Eventually they found me and took me to the police station. My father was already waiting there with a gun, and when he saw Relampago he took a shot at him. I threw myself between them and the bullet grazed my head. I still have traces of that scar. Relampago also tried three times to kill my father. Later he had no contact with my parents at all and even prevented me from sending them any money. My mother refused to give us permission to marry, but in the end my father talked her out of it. You see, at that time a girl was considered a tramp if she lived with a man outside of marriage.

The couple lived with Relampago's mother for the first two years. Then they began performing together again, going on tour, but still spending a great deal of their time in Madrid. One day Antonia Mercé ("La Argentina") saw Carmen dance in the "Romeo" theater there. It was the mid '20s and she was out scouting for talent for a new production of *El Amor Brujo*, a ballet Manuel de Falla had written a few years earlier for the singer Pastora Imperio. He had worked a lot with her mother, La Mejorana, the famous 19th-century cantaora and bailaora. But the first performances of the ballet, under Pastora Imperio's direction, had been disappointing.

She played a melody for me and asked, "What would you dance to this?" "Bulería, of course!" I told her. That was the "fofolé." The other flamenco dance for ballet, which I then danced, had a samba rhythm.

La Argentina was one of the greatest classical Spanish dancers. She asked La Joselito to teach her some flamenco dances. "In exchange I wanted her to show me how to play the castanets; she was an expert. So we traded. That was how I came to teach her the alegría and the tanguillo."

The first performance at the Opéra Comique in Paris with La Joselito was a big hit. The Paris Opera added the ballet to its repertoire and La Argentina signed a contract for a major European tour for the entire company. They appeared in every large city in Germany, but when in Dresden Carmen received a telegram reporting her father's death:

Someone handed it to me right before the performance. My husband was furious. And I was just wiped out. But then it was time to go on. Did I ever dance! And cry. Cried and danced. Even La

Argentina, who didn't particularly care for me and never gave me any compliments, said that night, "You'll never again dance as well as you danced tonight!"

La Argentina had mixed feelings about her lead dancer's huge success in the company. "She was incredibly jealous and often downright mean to me."

When she was invited to take her ballet to America, she chose Vicente Escudero to go with them. But one day, quite unexpectedly, a Russian (most flamenco troupe managers in those days were Russians) knocked on La Joselito's door in Paris. He brought a message from La Argentina: Could La Joselito join her for a cocktail?

> I was very suspicious because, after all, we'd had a complete falling out. I went but I took my husband along. I asked her what she wanted from me and she said she would like me to dance in a ballet based on Albéniz's music, *Triana.* My husband exploded. "First you complain about Carmen in the opera and now you want her for your ballet!" And I said, "You ridiculed me in America and now you come to me only because you know your ballet won't make it unless I dance in it." Then she took me aside and said, "Listen, you have your whole life ahead of you, but I'm nearing the end. Pretty soon I won't be able to dance any more." But no sooner had I danced successfully in this ballet than she pulled a long face and said to me again, "Listen, I've got a name to protect, leave the triumphs to me. You still have your whole career ahead of you, for me it's almost over, please try to understand!"

It was true. A few years later during a performance in Bayonne, La Argentina dropped dead.

La Joselito and her husband then lived in Paris. Although they had property and savings in Spain, they were not allowed to return after the Civil War. Relampago being a Republican, they received many dignitaries from the Spanish Republic in their apartment: for example, Franco's brother Ramón, a passionate opponent of Franco. About Relampago Carmen had her doubts:

> He hit me once because I cursed at him: "You call yourself a Republican, but at home you act like a real Facist." You see, he made my life pretty tough. He meant everything to me, he taught me how to read and write, but after he died I learned that he had been cheating on me the whole time. He always treated me like a little girl; I only became a woman after his death.

In Paris, La Joselito scored her next success in the opera *La illustre fragora* by Laparra, in which she was expected to perform the only dance she had ever been taught, the zapateado. She had danced it in private, of course, but never in public. Quite by chance, Antonio de Bilbao, who had taught her the dance, was in Paris at the time and encouraged her to accept the challenge. And so, at the Paris Opera, dressed in an elegant grey and black dress, in front of a backdrop depicting the famous Sevillian café cantante "Kursaal," she danced the zapateado for the first time in public. The audience gave her a standing ovation and Antonio, who was there that night, added his personal congratulations. That was the last time she saw him. He died a few years later in Barcelona.

La Joselito and her husband Relampago began making solo appearances in Paris, putting on a two-part show, one part flamenco and the other part Spanish regional dances with piano accompaniment. The first performance was held in the *Salle Gaveau.* They took this show all over Europe and when the Second World War broke out, they flew to South Africa, then to Scandanavia. The Germans sent them to Poland and Czechoslovakia. They had to perform three times a week for German troops in Paris at the Moulin Rouge, the Olympia and the Normandy Theater, as well as at the elegant Hotel George V where the German generals were headquartered.

> We were paid well and got soap, rice and flour. All the Jewish merchants on our street, the rue Levis, knew this and fortunately understood our predicament. I only took advantage of our position twice (I could do this because the general was a real aficionado and spoke pretty good Spanish): Once to free my brother, who was in a prison camp in southern France, and another time to free a Jewish neighbor.

After the war, they toured Turkey and Greece and spent a year and a half in Australia. After returning from Australia, Relampago became very ill. They nevertheless went through with a tour of Yugoslavia that had already been scheduled and afterwards spent a month in Opatija at Tito's country villa. Then began the six long years of Relampago's illness. Since neither he nor Carmen had health insurance, she spent everything they had earned to care for her sick husband. Convinced that Carmen could not live without him, Relampago kept an ax under his pillow so that he could take her with him when he died. "One day I took the ax away from him and hid it so well I never found it again."

Following her husband's death in 1956, Carmen, then middle-aged, was on the verge of a breakdown, her career as good as finished. Two years later, the singer Jacinto Almaden introduced her to the young guitarist Pedro Soler and his sister Isabel, who was studying dancing. Together with the guitarist Pepe de Badajoz and Rosa Montoya, Ramón Montoya's niece, they went on tour together. In 1967 she made a recording with Pedro Soler and two singers, Pepe El de la Matrona and Jacinto Almaden, that won the Charles Cros Award and is still considered one the great collaborations in flamenco history. Paris rediscovered its star of the '20s and '30s when this same group performed that year at *Le petit Odéon*, which was still being managed by Jean-Louis Barrault. Claude Sarraute reported in *Le Monde* (June 1, 1967):

> She has lost little of her incredible agility, and her vitality, rather than decreasing has become concentrated, compressed. The wrinkles on her obstinate brow underscore the characteristic gypsy dignity of her turns, of her hammering heels. In the circle of her raised arms, only the brief smile of a bright note relieves the strict sobriety of an art whose authenticity she preserves as a living conservatory, by insistently returning to its origins.

Since 1975, La Joselito has lived in Toulouse, the French home of Spanish Republicans, where she trains young dancers. Trying to teach flamenco has led La Joselito to struggle long and hard for the first time with this craft she knows so well. Breaking a step down into its various components, for instance, demands a great deal of self-discipline, and during her first few teaching sessions, her temper sometimes got the better of her. A step that started slowly became a thundering sequence that simply left her students bewildered.

Bailaoras and Bailaores

Everything La Joselito teaches, she knows inside out, so I turned to her to learn about some of the famous figures in flamenco. This was a delicate matter because La Joselito is a very severe, "biased" if you will, critic. She measures flamenco against the standard of an age that with good reason is called "golden." Thus she sometimes thinks she sees in an Atahualpa Yupanqui or some other great artist of today, the real "hero" of flamenco, the "duende."

Some of the greatest flamenco artists played an important part in La Joselito's life and are therefore already familiar to the reader. Nonetheless, their names bear repeating in the following chronology. Although these names are well known to aficionados, the layman can take this opportunity to become more familiar with them.

Over 100 years ago, two famous women were dancing in Seville in addition to Rosario Monje (La Mejorana): Trinidad La Cuenca and Salud La Hija del Cieglo (the blindman's daughter). Antonio Vidal studied under them. His father came from Bilbao, where Antonio was born (thus "de Bilbao"), and his mother from Seville. In La Joselito's opinion, he was the finest of all flamenco dancers. He was extremely popular and toured all over the world. His vast repertory included Spanish regional as well as flamenco dances.

The two greatest female flamenco dancers from the "Edad de Oro"

La Singla

Carmen Amaya (left)

often appeared on stage together: Juana Vargas La Macarrona, who was quite corpulent and danced publicly until her death at age 90 (she was killed in the Civil War), and Magdalena Seda La Malena. La Joselito believes that there are none better than these, but of the two, La Macarrona was by far the more expert, the more intriguing. Today La Joselito's admiration for these two dancers is shared: "There remain the two most famous, the queens of flamenco dancing, La Malena and La Macarrona. These two exceptional women, both representatives of the era of great flamenco passions, were very controversial figures. Both were gypsies and very fat, but they performed with an incomparable presence" (Udaeta, p. 27).

Juan Sanchez Estampio, Ramirez, Francisca Gonzales La Quica and her husband Francisco Léon Frasquillo were all dancing at the same time as La Malena and La Macarrona. As a young girl, La Joselito met the aging dancer Rafael Vega, who danced more than just flamenco, and José Molina, who sometimes invited her to his dance academy in Barcelona.

Antonia Mercé La Argentina, who died young in 1936, was for La Joselito a "bailarina" of genius, but not a "bailaora."

When asked about such well-known names as Vicente Escudero,

Antonio Ruis Soler (Antonio) and Antonio Gades, who in recent years has received a great deal of publicity, La Joselito's reply was, "Are you talking about flamenco or Spanish ballet?" Nonetheless, Vicente Escudero enlarged the flamenco dance repertory with the siguiriya. He loved to talk about how Surrealism had influenced him and he became the darling of New York audiences after La Argentina introduced him there in the '30s. It was also in New York that Antonio achieved his greatest fame, and indeed his dance style was sometimes truly acrobatic. Roger Mindlin wrote of him:

> It seems that of all the Spanish dancers, "Antonio" has borrowed most heavily from the classical ballet, adapting its forms to the Spanish dance. The characteristic leaps with which he besieges his partner (Florencia Pérez, known as "Rosario") are reminiscent of a classical "pas de deux."

If this is true, we then have to ask ourselves how Mindlin arrived at the following paradoxical conclusion: "Nonetheless, he retained the essence of "jondo" and "flamenco" perfectly in all his creations (Mindlin, p. 39)."

This kind of hyperbole pushes La Joselito's tolerance to its limits. She cites the tempestuous Carmen Amaya as one of the persons most responsible for the vulgarization of flamenco dancing. La Joselito swears she has said this to her face, "which was a very dangerous thing to do because she always had her whole gypsy clan backing her up." There is no doubt that Amaya, who was this century's most popular dancer, had an unerring sense of rhythm and was true to her naturally fiery temperament. She came, moreover, from a highly talented gypsy family living in Barcelona (her father was the guitarist El Chino and her aunt Juana Amaya, who danced under the name La Faraona, was a well-known dancer). But she herself never had any contact with the great historic figures of flamenco and thus developed a highly personalized style of dancing, the vitality of which obscured its lack of adherence to any traditional concept of style. She loved the typical gypsy dances. She danced traditional flamenco with great vehemence and a very forceful zapateado. "Flamenco speaks powerfully, not because it relies on nervousness or frenzy, but because its movements are understated and its posture is controlled," says La Joselito, whose concept of flamenco differs totally from that of Carmen Amaya. The latter's dance style clearly displayed qualities that did not measure up to the highest traditions of flamenco, and for Carmen Joselito that is the sole criterion. Judgments like these may seem overly harsh, but this is part and parcel of the controversy that has always embroiled the flamenco world.

Antonio Singla (La Singla), a deaf mute, was hailed as Carmen Amaya's successor. Like Carmen Amaya, she grew up in the Somorostro slums on Barcelona's waterfront, and as a girl of 13 danced with Amaya in the gypsy film *Los Tarantos*. Her career was launched in the '60s at the Festival Flamenco Gitano but her greatest popularity came from outside Spain. Like her predecessor, La Singla also loved the dramatic "trouser dances," which exclude any flirtatious elements.

Regla Ortega, who performed in the cafés cantantes during the heydey of flamenco and who specialized in polos, tanguillos, gaditanos and tientos, came from the famous Ortega family. She made an innovative contribution to baile flamenco by converting tarantos and peteneras into dance forms. The flamenco scholar Caballero Bonald wrote of Regla Ortega that "her dance is like a ritual that is pure and majestic in every movement."

It is impossible to discuss flamenco dancing today without bringing up the name of Antonio Gades. Rarely has a flamenco artist achieved such a degree of international fame as that accorded Gades. He thinks of himself as following in the footsteps of Antonio and Vicente Escudero, but he owes his big break to his excellent collaboration with the Spanish director Carlos Saura on the films *Blood Wedding* and *Carmen*. His international fame rests mainly on his impeccable staging and the almost scientifically geometric precision of his choreography: Nothing is overlooked, from the raising of an eye to the color of shoes. This results in a show of such incomparable quality that one almost forgets that the purpose, flamenco dancing, is so tightly controlled that almost nothing of it remains. But audiences grown weary of tourist spectacles suddenly sit up and take notice because at last someone is offering them truly significant stagecraft. Moreover, Gades is a genius at interweaving all sorts of cherished clichés into his productions. Emotional femininity and tough manliness, passion and dance, the omnipresent Church and olive-skinned gypsies. Yet this is done with such an unerring sense of esthetics that even the more skeptical members of the audience, who know that his ballets deal in clichés, are won over. Success is guaranteed! But flamenco—the lonely, personal, spontaneous expression of an artist—is lost in the telling.

One bright spot in Gades' work is Christina Hoyos. Despite the rigorousness of the choreography, to which she must acquiesce, she occasionally succeeds in giving us a glimpse of what real inspiration means to flamenco.

Whether it be the commercialism of show business or the academic perfectionism of Gades' ballets—flamenco is losing out. Only a few have managed to escape these twin perils as completely as a company from Seville called "La Cuadra," under the direction of Salvador Tavora. Himself of gypsy heritage by way of his grandmother, Tavora identifies strongly with the history of Andalusia's gypsies. The "Cuadra" uses several interesting concepts to show audiences aspects of flamenco that have been lost and forgotten in the course of its downward slide into slick entertainment.

One of these concepts is that flamenco has its roots in the working life of Andalusians and that dramatic elements can be derived from that fact. While the only accompaniment to the blacksmith's song, the martinete, was once the sound of the hammer striking the anvil, Juan Romero, one of the "Cuadra's" dancers, might dance it to the strong, grinding rhythm of a cement mixer or the sound of heavy, iron chains. These "instruments" are components of staging that modern dramaturgy is beholden to and do not violate the integrity of flamenco.

Behind the "Cuadra's" attempt to overcome superficiality in flamenco and to create a new awareness of its folk heritage lie considerations which must seem suspect to traditional performers. But theirs is perhaps the modern way of maintaining originality and authenticity, or at least referring to them. In any case, "La Cuadra" is a welcome departure from almost everything else being done today.

El Farruco, who is well over 50, is also a contemporary dancer worth noting. He heads a company from Seville which maintains a strong sense of flamenco traditions. Of the same generation and with a dance studio in the same city, Enrique El Cojo (called "The Cripple" because he limps) nevertheless holds quite the opposite opinion: "Flamenco doesn't need to rely on tradition. Flamenco is anarchy . . ." (Lartigue, p. 40). Matilde Coral was born in 1935 in Triana, the gypsy section of Seville, and runs a large dance academy there. She says of Enrique El Cojo that he is no longer capable of training flamenco dancers, but that he knows how to give the power of dance, the "poison" it needs: "His infirmity seems to have sharpened his wits" (Lartigue, p. 40). In her opinion, there are hardly any true flamenco dancers left. She refers to herself and Antonio Gades as mere "bailarines."

Two dancers from Coral's era who showed great promise are now all but forgotten: Antonio La Singla, whom we have already mentioned, and Micaela Flores La Chunga, a niece of Carmen Amaya, who often dances her frenzied version of flamenco barefoot. These days she appears at the "Café de Chinitas" in Madrid, but whether her craft has ever lived up to her image is questionable.

The most promising new talent has been the young and attractive Manuela Carrasco, a gypsy from Triana. Her wildness and powerful footwork were probably inspired by Carmen Amaya, but she also knows how to effectively use stillness, pauses and understatement. Her troupe, in which her husband accompanies her on the guitar, includes another important name: the dancer and choreographer Manolo Soler. Not being a gypsy, he is probably best classified as a flamenco avantgardist who experiments with the rhythmic elements of this art.

El Guito, who is in his 40s and a master of the soleá, teaches flamenco in Madrid. He is a gypsy and was a student of the famed bailarina Pilar Lopez, who also knew how to dance flamenco extremely

Juana Vargas Amaya

well. Thus El Guito has managed to combine both "academia" and inspiration. He often dances with Merche Esmeralda, former prima ballerina of the Spanish National Ballet and member of Antonio's company.

Faíco also runs a dance academy in Madrid, teaching mainly the dance style of Carmen Amaya.

Other dancers worthy of note include Manuela Vargas, also Angelita Vargas, whose dance style is often a bit crude; the slightly academic Conchi Calero from Cordoba; the heavy-set Milagros, who is a cut above the rest of the tourist tablao with whom she dances in Barcelona; and finally La Joselito's only professional student, Isabel Soler, who at 44 resumed her career after being retired for many years.

I should also mention Mario Maya, whose highly individualistic style has distinguished him as one of the few contemporary dancers who feels beholden to strict flamenco traditions. He too uses theater as a vehicle for his sober, unadorned and abstract dances. Among his themes are the harsh social conditions under which the Andalusian gypsies have lived. Yet the persuasive power and deep tension of his dances save them from being merely anecdotal. Maya does not rely on gloss, color-coordinated costumes and folklore; in fact he allows nothing to distract from the dance itself.

In addition, he is constantly searching out promising young people, whom he then introduces to the public through his company, "Teatro gitano andaluz." This was how audiences came to know Juana Amaya from Moron de la Frontera, who was only 16 years old when he discovered her, and 22-year-old Carmen Cortez from Barcelona, who makes beautiful use of her arms.

Under the guidance of a master like Mario Maya, perhaps one of these young artists will some day be able to restore to flamenco the artistic universality it once had. La Joselito searches Spain at every chance she gets and never stops hoping.

GUITARRA FLAMENCA

Ehrenhard Skiera
Bernhard-Friedrich Schulze

Thanks to performances by Spanish flamenco companies and guitar soloists abroad, as well as millions of recordings, television and radio appearances, in the last few decades flamenco has become known the world over. Solo flamenco guitar has enjoyed a particular popularity due to the technical brilliance and virtuosity of such performances. The essence of flamenco music is conveyed through its melodic and dancelike rhythmic elements, and the guitar is suited like no other instrument to capture these qualities.

But in the last few years Spanish and non-Spanish guitarists alike have abandoned the profound character of flamenco in order to play to the gallery. Too little attention is paid to the fact that flamenco, particularly flamenco song, articulates personal and social aspirations which are deeply rooted in the history of Andalusia and its sorrows, the *pena andaluza*. Deriving from and guided by the cante, flamenco guitar music has developed a specific esthetic that in turn influences playing technique, concept of sound and even the instrument's construction. Lost in all this virtuosity, moreover, is the fact that the various *toques* (flamenco pieces and techniques for the guitar), are based on clear melodic and rhythmic basic patterns, which are not immediately accessible to Central Europeans and North Americans, who are more inclined to hear harmonically. But the richness of this music is revealed to the listener only if he is aware—consciously or unconsciously—of these specific structures and these esthetic factors. Indeed, the flamenco guitarist depends on this awareness to infuse his personal interpretation with the right musical quality.

Esthetics, History, and Construction of the Flamenco Guitar

(Bernhard-Friedrich Schulze)

I first went to Andalusia, the birthplace of flamenco guitar, in the early 1970s to obtain the most authentic instruction possible in this folk art. My teacher in Málaga, the tocaor (flamenco guitarist) Paco Soler, handed me a surprise in the very first lesson. Challenged to demonstrate the level of my knowledge and preparation, I played a *granaina* on an authentic flamenco guitar, playing the exact notes I had taken from a written score, and using a technique learned from reading a textbook on flamenco guitar. My teacher was somewhat dismayed and asked me if that was really a granaina I was playing, and if so where did I find those notes. In order to explain his doubts, he then played some passages himself. Although I was able to recognize the characteristic figures from music I had read, I was surprised at how different they seemed when I actually heard them.

This experience and this scene demonstrate the typical starting point at which every foreigner finds himself when setting about learning to play flamenco guitar and understanding this musical heritage. This "typical situation" is no less than the confrontation between a concept of sound growing out of the musical traditions of Central Europe and the concept of sound authentic to flamenco. With this in mind, I have attempted to examine from various angles the unique esthetics of flamenco guitar playing.

Expressiveness and the Sound Ideal of the Flamenco Guitar

There is a wide range of music for flamenco guitar. The question is: What directions for playing this music actually enable a non-Andalusian guitarist to reproduce the notes in such a way as to give his playing an authentic *aire flamenco*, its "flavor" and expressiveness?

As is well understood, this is a universal problem faced by performers on every instrument. Between the written music of any kind and the intended sound there lies a gap that can only be bridged by very specific, culturally imparted performance practices and interpretations. Bridging this gap becomes more difficult the older or more culturally isolated a given music is. Thus a singer with a secure voice and knowledge of notation but lacking the appropriate experiential background and ear training, will probably not be able to sing, say, a Gregorian chorale from 10th-century Europe or 20th-century Afro-American blues correctly.

In the case of flamenco music, this problem is compounded by three added factors:

1. The beginning flamenco guitarist is misled by the notation typical of the literature for *guitarra flamenca de concierto*, (solo flamenco guitar). It often looks like a classical concerto score which leads him to play the familiar classical sounds of the concert guitar, and this misunderstanding is only reinforced by the pleasant-sounding results.

2. Flamenco music (and this is especially true for the guitar) contains numerous improvisational elements that cannot, as such, be

written down. In *guitarra flamenco de concierto,* previously acquired *falsetas* and *rasgueados* are combined in quite creative and original ways in an improvisational style that is typically quite traditional. The *guitarra flamenca de acompañamiento* (flamenco guitar as an accompanying instrument) supports the song and/or dance, but adds original touches in a kind of dialogue which depends upon the mood or feel of what is happening at the moment.

Interestingly, this practice of varying and combining melodic and rhythmic-harmonic patterns (falsetas and rasgueados, respectively) is similar in many ways to the practices found in Arabic and Indian music.

3. Traditionally, flamenco guitar is taught and learned by listening, i.e. the student imitates the teacher's playing style note for note. The teacher and student also play together, either taking turns and comparing the two versions or playing in unison with the intent of achieving the highest possible degree of similarity.

This way of learning only adds to an already complicated situation: Scoring for typical playing techniques like the rasgueado was, until recently, often faulty and somewhat arbitrary because no written tradition existed, and what was available in the way of a traditional system of notation was not put to full use.

The native Andalusian guitarist is guided by daily experience and quite unconsciously absorbs the idiom of flamenco guitar. He hears the music regularly (live and on radio and TV), is in contact with other guitarists and aficionados, and is relatively unburdened by concerns about notation. His European counterpart, on the other hand, is faced with a twofold problem. First, he finds virtually no signposts for producing the particular tone of the flamenco guitar in the score itself. Second, simply listening to the various musical *estilos* (styles) is uncertain at best and does not enable him to draw conclusions or distinguish among them.

In view of all this, it seems important to pause here and attempt to describe the world of sound and the esthetics associated with *aire flamenco.*

Sound Concept and Ideal

The saying that guitar and cante belong together "like fingernail and cuticle" points up a central issue in flamenco music and indeed in all European music.

From times immemorial, instrumental music has served as accompaniment to dancing and singing, that is to say, it has always been in a more or less dependent position. Beginning in Europe in the 16th century, however, instrumental music was slowly emancipated from vocal music. Music written for voices began to be played on instruments and was in turn increasingly influenced by specifically instrumental ways of thinking and playing. Yet this early instrumental music was still very much like vocal music in its phrasing, progression, thematic development, etc.

In flamenco music this development proceeded as follows: In the beginning (the 18th century at the latest), songs were sung without any guitar accompaniment; later (beginning of the 19th century) the guitar was used to accompany songs; and finally (second half of the 19th century) the solo guitar was played in concert.

Obviously, the example of the European-Spanish concert guitar played a crucial role in this, if you will, delayed development. Whereas Christian Spain was completely in step with European musical developments—consider, for example, the contributions to the European tradition made by Spanish organ and harpsichord music during the time of Charles V and Philipp II—music in Arabic Spain was proceeding in a quite different direction. It must be borne in mind that the cultural traditions of Andalusia, ruled for centuries by the Moors, were strongly influenced by Arabic musical culture and performance practices, which does not include music for solo instruments. It should also be noted that the Iraqi musician Zyriab exerted a profound effect on the way in which music was taught at the court of Córdoba in the 9th century, and that Arabs continued to teach music in Christian schools even after the Reconquista (1492).

But it is the esthetic aspect of this development that is so critical: The question of how much influence the sound of flamenco singing has had on the sound of the flamenco guitar.

If we look more closely at how the guitarra flamenca de acompañamiento functions in the cuadro flamenco (flamenco guitar as an ensemble instrument in a flamenco unit including song, dance, guitar and jaleo), it is evident that a constant exchange takes place between rasgueado sections and punteado sections. Rasgueado alerts the singer to the rhythm, pitch, harmony and indicates when the song begins and ends. The melodic punteado parts (puntear = to strike individual notes), on the other hand, take up the song, imitate it, comment on it, and challenge the singer, but at the same time provide him with a rest and the room to regain his concentration. Mindful then of the function and practice of the punteado, we can see how extensively the tone of the flamenco guitar has been influenced by the song and how it is oriented to the latter.

If we try to define more closely cante's special timbre, which differs so radically from the familiar classical bel canto with its artful bridging between vocal registers, two things strike us: First, the notes are colored by small, enharmonic intervals, which occasionally sound off-key or "impure," and secondly, there is a tremendous diversity of vocal

124

registers or colors, ranging from husky and guttural through full and velvety all the way to a forced falsetto.

Both these observations can equally well be made of Arabic-Islamic music and language. Thus the "impurity" of sung notes harkens back to the highly differentiated 1/4, 1/2, 3/4, 1/1, 5/4 and 3/2 intervals of the Arabic tonal system; and the ideal Arabic singing voice has—thanks also to the language—a guttural character to it and sounds slightly forced.

Another characteristic, the impressive and varied dynamic formulation of the song and its vocal power, is due both to the emotional involvement with which the singer expresses the pena andaluza (pena = sorrow) and to the rather simple fact that the singer had to make himself audible to large audiences—long before there were such things as microphones and amplifiers.

It should also be noted that the phonetic aspects of the language are often skillfully turned into music and then incorporated into a song's delivery, for instance the invented flamenco sounds called *farfullos,* such as "lerele," "trajilitraji," and "tirititran," the lamenting "ay, ay" (*quejíos*) or the extreme stretching of individual vowels (*jipío*).

Flamenco Tone Quality (Timbre)

But how can the emotional coloration, registration and dynamics of song, with their immediate impact, be imitated on the guitar? Leaving aside for the moment the unique construction of the flamenco guitar itself (which has been modified to serve its special purpose), the timbre of a melody can be manipulated by varying a) the striking point, b) the striking angle, and c) what is used to strike the strings.

a) The flamenco guitarist usually plays his instrument as closely as possible to the bridge, which as we know communicates the vibration of the strings to the soundboard. This gives the notes a certain *harsh, rasping* quality. Of course, the exact striking point also depends on the length of the freely vibrating part of the string (frequency, pitch). But normally the instrument is played between the sound hole and the bridge.

b) The string is struck or "pushed" downward toward the soundboard—rather than plucked parallel to the soundboard as in the classical *tirando* (tirar = to pull). This technique is known by every concert guitarist as the support stroke. The striking finger *i* (index finger) or *m* (middle finger) is caught and supported by the next lowest string, or in the case of the thumb (*p*), by the next highest. In Spanish this technique is called *apoyando* (apoyar = to support); it produces *full,* prolonged, and sometimes (if the strings vibrate gently against the frets) *slightly percussive* tones.

c)   The strings are struck or pushed by a combination of *callo* (fingertips) and *uña* (fingernails). Fingernails make ideal picks, as they can transmit various signals to the player, enabling him to produce clearly contoured, intense, and at times plaintive tones.

Lastly, there is the technique of *rasgueado,* in which "whirling" fingernails go unchecked by the fingertips. It creates extremely sharp harmonic and rhythmically percussive accents.

The typical flamenco sound is achieved when all three ways of playing are combined. When doing so, it is important to keep the flamenco song uppermost in mind and not be afraid of playing loudly.

Moreover, in contrast to classical guitar technique, the thumb mainly plays *apoyando,* even in the case of arpeggios and tremolos.

The curvatures of the nail and the physiology of the individual hand must be precisely coordinated to render a technically good performance. Since this is not always easy to accomplish, a couple of suggestions are offered.

1.   Regardless of individual differences, the nail has three curved planes: (1) seen from above, it is arched lengthwise over the finger bone, (2) seen from below, it is rounded parallel to the fingertip when well manicured, and (3) seen from the side, it curves downward like a claw if left untrimmed.

2.   To strike correctly, the nail always contacts the string at two points. In the case of the index and middle fingers, these are the two intersecting points between nail and fingertip. But for the thumb, since it is used at an angle, these points lie between the thumbnail and edge of the thumb and the tip of the thumbnail.

In any case, the nails must be kept fairly long so that they can be filed to the correct shape. This is particularly true of the thumbnail.

Interestingly enough, Zyriab played his guitar with a plectrum, and the Arabic Ud lute is also played with a plectrum.

The organization of pitches and intervals of the flamenco guitar follows the European model, i.e. the octaves are subdivided by frets into the twelve familiar, well-tempered half steps. As a consequence flamenco guitars are severely limited when it comes to imitating the Arabic elements of the cante.

Animation (Aire Flamenco) and Expressiveness

Flamenco guitar music alternates between the rhythmic and harmonic rasgueado and the melodic punteado. Both of these basic elements are intensely and expressively shaped by the type of intonation we have mentioned. But in the end the real "magic," the fascinating aspect of flamenco, is caused by the constant interplay and alternation of these melodic and rhythmic elements.

If, for example, the rhythmic-harmonic rasgueado from the soleá is played, a flamenco singer knows not only that he is singing a soleá and when he will sing each verse, but the listener immediately identifies with the wealth of soleares melodies he has heard before. Rasgueados open the gates, so to speak, to release the falsetas and close the gates to signify their end, establishing at the same time a point of rest.

The presentation of the falsetas by the rasgueados is understood by virtue of active listening, which, as we know, enables one to both antici-pate and recollect familiar and repeated musical material. (It is difficult, for example, to break off a scale on the leading tone). Thus an actual superimposition of melody and melodic accents on the one hand, and compás and rhythmic accents on the other, can be heard in the falsetas by those acquainted with flamenco.

This explains why, for instance, the accent inherent in the melody of a soleá falseta can agree so perfectly with the soleá's cyclically recurring accentuation (see below), all of which gives the melody its subtle persuasive power:

However, the basic rhythmic pattern and the melodic accent may also differ—either because the "typing" (here a typical final phrase for the soleá) calls for it:

or because the player wants to reduce the rate of attrition of simple types (here part of a simple scale) by using syncopated accents:

The effect of this difference is quite exciting: The listener continues to sense the compás—which might also be marked by palmas—while at the same time he hears the melodic accents, which sometimes coincide with the accents of the basic rhythm and sometimes fall next to and between those of the compás. This polyrhythmic factor enormously intensifies the melody.

Jazz creates similar musical effects by using similar off-beat devices; the well-known uses of "drive" and "swing" also depend upon an energetic overlapping of two levels of accents.

But this analogy can only be carried so far because jazz uses none of the rhythmic patterns associated with authentic compás. Compás is more like the Indian "tala" or the Arabic "wazn," which also employ long, regularly recurring rhythmic cycles (see below).

History and Development of Playing Techniques

I now turn to the technique of playing flamenco guitar and its technically correct and musically appropriate use.

These two factors are intimately related, since playing technique is really nothing more than the physical execution of a mental concept, while musical expressiveness depends largely on perfecting technique. Let us say then that technique and musical expressiveness operate reciprocally and have had, moreover, a quite stormy history. Improvements in methodology and technique not infrequently lead to musical decline. Thus if technique is used as an end in itself or if the inherent dynamics of the music being played have not been thoroughly mastered, a scale may be started too quickly, which leads the music away from or contrary to the particular musical context. The melodic expression of a flamenco falseta, for example, then loses all significance and degenerates into mere ornament or worse yet, finger exercises.

It seems expedient, therefore, to clarify what the musical and esthetic purpose of the basic techniques originally was. To do this I will trace their development from the beginnings in the early 19th century, when the guitar was only an accompanying instrument, through the integration and overemphasis of classical playing techniques in the latter part of the 19th century, at which time flamenco still retained its own established set of esthetics, up to the new emergent stylistic and esthetic syntheses of the second half of this century.

Legendary Masters

Even though the Spanish guitar was extremely popular in Andalusia at the end of the 18th century, it had not yet been used as an instrument to accompany the cante. The role of providing rhythmic backup was traditionally filled by palmas, taconeos (see p. 151), etc. It should be noted that a guitar was at that time a very expensive instrument for ordinary peasants to own, yet they were the keepers of the song.

In the first third of the 19th century the Spanish guitar was used sporadically as an accompanying instrument (the flamenco guitar was only introduced in the mid-19th century), but flamenco guitar playing only really came into its own in 1842 with the advent of the cafés can-

Pepino Salazar

tantes. These cafés offered guitarists a forum for communication, by which they could learn from one another. The public nature of the cafés also encouraged playing of more professional quality.

Francisco Rodriguez from Granada, known as El Murciano (1795–1848), was a famous performer from this early period before the cafés cantantes, and is the first flamenco guitarist known by name. Playing technique at this time was "limited" chiefly to the rasgueado and the use of the thumb to play the melody. The frequent characterization of this method as "primitive" obviously overlooks the extremely skillful use of the thumb, which many a professional today might well learn.

The appearance of El Maestro Patiño (1830–1900) from Cádiz and Antonio Perez (1835–1900) from Seville takes us into the flamenco café period. Both viewed guitar playing purely as an accompaniment to song and dance.

This view changed with Patiño's master pupil from Cádiz, Francisco Sánchez, known as Paco el Barbero (1840–1910). He was the first in the history of flamenco to give solo guitar performances. The reasons for this were complex. First, it is much more difficult and at the same time less glamorous to accompany a famous singer or dancer. In addition to mastering guitar technique, the player has to be thoroughly and widely grounded in the songs and dances being performed, and must be able to respond instantly to the singer's or dancer's improvisations. To top it off, the glory usually goes not to the guitarist, but to the interpreter of the song or dance. By contrast, a solo performance of falsetas gives the guitarist the opportunity to express his own musical style, and at the same time show off his technical and musical skills.

So it was that El Barbero turned a page on a completely new chapter in the rapidly changing history of flamenco guitar: Borrowing and adapting classical and concert practices to flamenco, in short, the *aflamencar* ("flamencoization") of classical techniques.

Francisco Diaz, known as Paco Lucena (1855–1930), from Córdoba was the first to introduce such techniques as the *picado*, the three-fingered arpeggio and the three-fingered trémolo.

Javier Molina (1868–1956) from Jerez de la Frontera, who studied with El Barbero, and the famous Manuel Serrapi from Seville, who was known as El Niño Ricardo (1909–1972) and who studied under Molina, were two of the great flamenco guitarists from this period. With the arrival on the scene of Ramón Montoya (1880–1949) from Madrid, Lucena's pioneering work of integrating classical techniques was systematically advanced and brought to its conclusion. Montoya's admiration for Javier Molina's music and his intimacy with the music of the classical masters Francisco Tárrega (1852–1909) and Miguel Llobet (1878–1938) were reflected in the following new developments: the four-fingered tremolo, the introduction of complex arpeggio techniques, greater use of the picado, and finally, stronger and more difficult left hand work. This, together with Montoya's huge success in Paris in 1936, focused international attention on the guitarra flamenca de concierto.

A complete master of all these techniques was Agustín Castellón (1913–) from Pamplona, whose stage name was Sabicas. He too contributed enormously to making the flamenco guitar widely known outside of Spain. His record called *Flamenco Puro,* which might be described as his artistic legacy, demonstrates that he was a brilliant master of the solo flamenco guitar, while his work with the dancer, Carmen Amaya (1913–1963), reveals his skills as an accompanist.

This willingness to turn the flamenco guitar into such a technically demanding solo and accompanying instrument was greeted with skepticism by some guitarists, among them Pedro del Valle from Jerez (1894–1964), a student of Molina who performed under the name Perico el del Lunar. He did not approve of these developments, but rather dedicated himself entirely to the study of cante and baile. It should be mentioned here that he collaborated on the first great *Antologia del Cante Flamenco.* Perico had little patience with these new techniques, as is true of Diego Amaya Flores (Diego del Gastor) from Morón de la Frontera (1906–1973).

The period after the Spanish Civil War and World War II was largely dominated by the style of performers like Niño Ricardo and Sabicas. Guitarists still active today, including Francisco Sanchez Gomez (stage name: Paco de Lucía) (1947–), Victor Monge (Serranito), (1942–), Juan Martín (1942–), Paco Peña (1942–) and Manolo Sanlúcar (1944–), to name but a few, are largely playing in the styles of these two great masters.

Before I move on to the movements involving the younger generation, I will examine in a more detailed way the historical developments associated with these masters.

The Integration of Flamenco and Classical Guitar Techniques

Long before Paco Lucena and Ramón Montoya introduced classical elements into flamenco guitar practice, an esthetic of the cante was in place. Taking its cue from this esthetic, early guitar technique had successfully brought a balanced exchange between rasgueado and punteado into being. In actual playing practice this translated into the powerful, extroverted movement of the "half-open fist," typical of the rasgueado, and the vigorous, introverted technique of the punteado, using thumb and index or middle finger in the apoyando manner.

When the use of the ring finger was added, the three fingers (in the case of trémolos and arpeggios) had to play tirando, but the thumb had not yet been integrated into the tirando stroke. Had the use of the thumb been changed, a softer and more concert-like tone would have resulted and thus have been a foreign esthetic, a foreign musical entity. Secondly, the hand, whose movements were conditioned by and built around playing flamenco, was more or less accustomed to the thumb playing apoyando, i.e. the hand had developed a particular feeling when playing that players were reluctant to give up without good reason.

The preference in flamenco for melody became even more pronounced because of Montoya's innovations. He augmented the melodic two-part texture—already embodied in the tremolo and accentuated by the apoyando technique of the thumb—by adding yet another note to the rapid 16th-note repetitions of the upper part. This forced a marked contrast between the quiet apoyando in the lower part and the brilliant, now quadrupled, compressed and accelerated movement in the upper part. Instead of a quarter note in the lower part opposite *three* sixteenths in the upper part, there was now a quarter note in the lower part opposed to *four* sixteenth quintuplets in the upper part.

In the same way, retaining the apoyando technique of the thumb when playing an arpeggio, while increasing the virtuosity of the other fingers, emphasized the melodic dominance of the thumb, i.e. the three-

fingered arpeggio gave the melody a harmonic (broken chord), ornamental accompaniment, but without approaching a harmonic way of
thinking.

Esthetics of Contemporary Playing Techniques

Most of the great flamenco guitarists of today still come from
Andalusia, although they usually reside in the large metropolitan centers of Europe and North America, especially Madrid, London and New
York, and give concerts all over the world. While in the past, flamenco
was oriented more towards the musical traditions of south and east, its
esthetic impetus now is obtained primarily from the north and west.
Thus it is significant that Ramón Montoya, who was notable for introducing classical traditions into flamenco esthetics, came to Andalusia
from Madrid.

The influence of modern classical guitar esthetics continues to be
felt. Alongside the traditional "classical" flamenco style of a Niño
Ricardo or a Sabicas, a more concertante sound is beginning to establish
itself. This can be seen in the following trends:

1. The especially constructed (in terms of flamenco esthetics)
   flamenco guitar is being replaced in part by an instrument called
   the guitarra flamenca *negra*, which combines the construction
   principles of the flamenco guitar and the concert guitar (see
   below).

2. The *cajilla* (capo), once so popular and used to enable the
   guitarist to pitch his instrument to the singer and bring out the
   clear, metallic sound of the guitar, is not as much used, because
   the entire length of the finger-board is needed to execute all the
   new harmonies and playing techniques.

3. The traditional way of holding the guitar (see below) has
   changed somewhat, in that the left leg or left thigh is slightly
   raised to help support the guitar.

In addition, influences of completely different playing techniques
and musical esthetics have emerged, as seen, for example, in the famous
collaboration between Sabicas and Joe Beck or the tours made by Paco
de Lucías with the jazz-rock guitarists Larry Coryell, Al DiMeola and
John McLaughlin.

These departures have been variously called, flamenco-rock,
flamenco-jazzrock, classic-flamenco, etc. and are part of a larger, wide-
spread trend called "fusion music."

Yet despite these overall shifts, the "classical" style still persists,
practiced for example by Paco Peña, Juan Martín, and others. We must
add the name of Sabicas here as well, despite his occasional collaboration with Joe Beck. Even though most of these new movements have

focused on solo guitar performance, traditional flamenco guitar accompaniment is still very much alive and well. So today we hear both a progressive, logical development in flamenco playing technique and the emergence of all sorts of different playing styles.

Looking back on the developments described, it must be said that such fusions are not new, to flamenco music or to music in general. The fascination flamenco holds for Western civilization probably stems from the very fact that flamenco assimilated Indio-Arabic and other musical elements in Andalusia, thus making them more accessible to us.

Because the viewpoint of most in the West is necessarily based on European musical concepts and experience, the tendency is to focus on flamenco's classical and virtuoso elements; but as cante's more exotic aspects are gradually understood, the unfolding and the development of the history and esthetic of this music is more readily apparent.

It is not important to evaluate the very latest developments at this point, but we can be sure that the new flamenco guitar music, which is having an impact internationally and whose outlines are just taking shape, will some day require more complex definition and classification.

Construction and Function of the Flamenco Guitar

How have the esthetics of flamenco song and the role of accompaniment within the cuadro flamenco influenced the form and construction of the guitar in Andalusia?

To answer this question satisfactorily, it is necessary to focus on those musical and esthetic components and features of the flamenco guitar that differentiate it from its classical counterpart.

Antonio Torres and the Creation of the Flamenco Guitar

The kind of guitar developed by Antonio Torres (1817–1892), a guitar builder from Almería, actually had its antecedents in the 13th-century Spanish *guitarra latina,* which already had a feminine form and four strings, resembling the modern guitar. It is not essential for our purposes to determine who added the 5th and then the 6th strings—and when—questions which have not been satisfactorily answered at this writing.

What is important, however, is the fact that in the 13th century when the guitarra latina was used in the rest of Spain, the instrument indigenous to Andalusia was almond-shaped and called the *guitarra morisca.* This instrument had an extremely long neck with front pegs, but apparently no frets. These two forerunners of the modern guitar are thought to have been played in two different fashions: The latina employing the rasgueado technique, meaning that the thumb was used to play chords, and the morisca being played punteado style, that is, melodically. These were precisely the two techniques that were later combined in flamenco.

But the guitarra morisca was at first displaced by the lute, which in turn yielded to the advances made in the 18th century by the Spanish with the guitarra latina.

From the latter, Torres then created his famous prototype of the concert guitar, which demonstrated several advantages over previous models: A larger body, refinement of the structural or harmonic bars, mechanical tuning instead of rear pegs, etc. In the following, however, I deal only with his flamenco guitar.

Construction and Function of Flamenco Guitar Components

I list here those parts of the flamenco guitar that differ from the classical, together with a brief explanation of the esthetic and functional reasons for these differences.

1. The back and sides, i.e. most of the resonant body, are made of cypress rather than Brazilian rosewood. This is done to achieve a brighter sound more in keeping with cante flamenco. The lighter wood also makes the instrument easier to balance and is therefore better suited to the traditional playing position.

2. The bridge and bridge bone are lower, so that the vibrations of the strings are transmitted as directly as possible to the soundboard. This makes the tone sound sharper and more penetrating. The lower position of the strings not only makes left-hand action easier, but also produces a desirable percussive sound as the strings twang against the frets.

3. All the dimensions of the resonant body are slightly smaller. The smaller dimensions, especially the reduced depth of the sides, make the action of the instrument faster and thus better matched to the pace and agility of the singing.

4. The use of the *cejilla* (capo), which is almost unheard of in the concert guitar. This allows the guitarist to tune his instrument to the pitch of the singer without changing his left hand fingering and playing method. The cejilla also gives the instrument its characteristic "flamenco key" feeling. By raising the frequency and vibration of the strings, it also promotes a more rapid playing style.

5. A tapping plate is fastened to the top. *Golpe* (rhythmic accents) are tapped out on this plate. In addition, the extended ring finger of the right hand presses against the tapping plate when the melody is being played with the thumb; this counterpressure steadies the hand and helps control melodic intonation. In this case the tapping plate also serves as a protection for the soundboard.

6. The head has rear pegs rather than mechanical tuning. Aside from the esthetic aspect of building an instrument from homogeneous materials, in this case various woods, saving weight is the important factor here. This lighter weight gives the instrument better balance when being played in the traditional position.

7. The traditional flamenco playing position (see below) cannot properly be called a physical component of the flamenco guitar, yet it is so strongly associated with the instrument visually that it deserves to be included here with the other differentiating characteristics.

   This position has two advantages: (1) The left hand has easier access to the entire fingerboard because it is held closer to the body, and (2) the player can sit upright, without leaning his back against anything, which is far less tiring.

   But far more important is the fact that the right hand exercises greater strength and control in this position. Not only is the hand closer to the player but the angle of the arm is tighter and securely supported against the body of the guitar.

Generally speaking, the overall structure of the instrument has been largely determined by its role and function in the cuadro flamenco. In fact, the differences in points 1–3 were made to adapt the tone of the flamenco guitar to that of the cante, as is also true of point 4.

The difference noted in point 5 clearly was developed to bring the flamenco guitar into line with the rhythmic-percussive elements of flamenco, and the other rhythmic-percussive instruments.

Finally, points 6 and 7 speak to the advantages of a specific player posture relative to the endurance, virtuosity and dynamics of playing flamenco guitar.

The more recent guitarra flamenca negra results from combining structural features of both the flamenco and the concert guitar. It incorporates the dimensions of the flamenco guitar but the woods used in the concert model. The name *negra* comes from the dark colors of the woods, as opposed to *blanca*, which refers to the lighter shades of cypress. The purpose is to try to achieve a somewhat darker and mellower (more concertante) tone. Thus this newer instrument has been influenced more by the concert guitar than by the cante and the cuadro flamenco.

Musical Forms and Techniques for the Flamenco Guitar

(Ehrenhard Skiera)

Scales, Cadences, and Rhythms

In this section I present various characteristic musical features of flamenco. The musical examples offered are given in the usual guitar notation.

The melodic progression of most flamenco pieces moves in the Phrygian mode (example 1), the supertonic within the variations frequently functioning as a leading tone—that is, resolving downward—to the major chord on E (example 2). Another frequently used scale can be obtained by raising the mediant of the Phrygian mode (G-sharp example 3). The melodic character typical of songs from Islamic-Arabic regions (example 4) can now be heard in the alternation of minor, major and augmented seconds.

Fingering: p = thumb, i= index finger, m = middle finger, a = ring finger, c = little finger

These examples also emphatically illustrate the descending nature of the old Greek diatonic *systema teleion*. The Dorian mode in this system, aside from its direction, is similar to the later Phrygian church mode. But neither the late classic Dorian nor the medieval Phrygian included the use of variations of the supertonic and mediant in this way. Thus, there is really no accurate term for this key in flamenco music, although the word "Phrygian" has come into common usage. It should be remembered, however, that the scales used in Arabic and Indian music are identical with those used in flamenco. It is assumed that there are historic cross-connections here, but this assumption requires further musicological research to be sustained.

Characteristic of pieces from both melodic types is the use of a cadence (progression of chords) that goes from A minor to G and F major and finally to E major (example 5). Many passages or variations are based on this harmonic foundation (examples 6 and 7).

This imperfect (in terms of traditional harmony) cadence is frequently heard on the guitar in an altered form, and while this is due only to the structure of the instrument, it is precisely what gives it its peculiar charm: The G and F major chords are fingered incompletely so that strings 1 and 2 (e', b) remain open (example 8). When this cadence is transposed (example 9), it can be seen that this practice makes no sense either systematically or harmonically. Limited fingering of the B major chord causes the open first string (e') to vibrate as well.

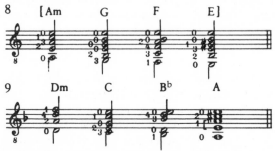

If passing chords in the cadence are used in these examples, the following passage from a taranta variation shows the limited fingering for the main chord of the tonic (in this case: F-sharp major, example 10).

The taranta, as a guitar solo, is based on the Phrygian scale raised by a major second and its correspondingly transposed principal cadence (B minor, A major, G major, F-sharp major). Its unique charm is due in part to the playing method mentioned above: Including open strings while playing melodies and chords. This piece, unlike its danced counterpart the taranto, allows a great deal of room for rhythmic interpretation.

In addition to the melodic and harmonic structures shown here, which are also used in transposed forms, there are a whole series of pieces whose musical foundations form a major scale and include the chord sequences (I, V⁷; I, IV, V⁷, I, etc.) identical to those used in traditional harmony. I have in mind here primarily those songs which originated in Andalusia, and were developed mainly by non-gypsies.

Based on their *compás* (rhythmic structure), flamenco pieces fall into three rather large groups. The table below presents the most important flamenco guitar solos classified according to their rhythmic unit of 12, 4 or 3 beats.

Although subtle rhythmic shadings exist in groups 2 and 3 (e.g. in the tientos, rumba flamenca, fandanguillos, etc.), an experienced European or American guitarist would have no trouble with them. This is not so with those in the first group, which without the benefit of preliminary rhythmic studies are difficult to master. The guitarist who is thoroughly familiar with the basic rhythms will then have access to many Spanish editions of music which, though they may contain beautiful variations, notate rhythms inaccurately and contain numerous other notational errors. Therefore, I would like to clarify the basic rhythms of the three sub-divisions of Group 1 to demonstrate how they are related

Group 1 12 beats	Group 2 4 beats	Group 3 3 beats
a) Notation: 4×3/4 or 3/8	Notation: 2/4 or 4/4	Notation: 3/4 or 3/8
Soleáres Caña Alegrías Romeras Caracoles Bulerías Cantiñas	Farruca Zambra Taranto Tientos Tanguillo Rumba flamenca Zapateado Colombianas Milonga Garrotín	Malagueñas Verdiales Tarantas Sevillanas Fandanguillos Granadinas Rondeña
b) Notation: 3/4 and 6/8 Siguiriyas Serranas		
c) Notation: 6/8 and 3/4 Peteneras Guajiras		

to each other rhythmically.

Group 1a: Example, Soleares

Four 3/4 measures (or four 3/8 measures) form a rhythmic unit of 12 beats, of which the 3rd, 6th, 8th, 10th and 12th are accented:

```
        >        >    >    >         >
1   2   3   4   5   6   7   8   9   10  11   12
```

Variations begin on the first beat, and after as many variations as are desired, the piece ends on the 10th beat of the rhythmic unit (example 11).

11

(Between the introduction and the close, examples 2, 6 and 7 can be inserted as variations [falsetas]).

All the pieces belonging to Group 1a are similarly structured, but in the case of bulerías, variations frequently begin on the 12th beat of the previous rhythmic unit (occasionally even on the 11th or 10th beat), which gives this piece its extraordinary dynamism (example 12).

12

Bulerías

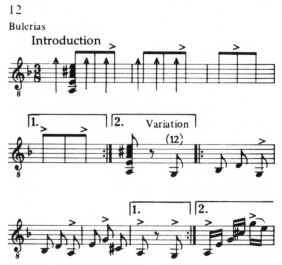

Group 1b: Example, Siguiriyas

In this case, accents are placed on the 1st, 3rd, 5th, 8th and 11th beat of the 12-beat rhythmic unit. By using 3/4 and 6/8 time, the notation is in keeping with the rhythm:

12a

The piece and its variations begin on the second quarter note in 3/4 time (which is the same as the 1st beat of the rhythmic unit) or on the first eighth-note in 6/8 time (which corresponds to the 5th beat of the rhythmic unit). In the latter case, the beginning of the rhythmic unit is imagined or completed by tapping the quarter notes twice (*golpe,* see below). After any number of variations, the piece then ends on the 10th or 11th beat of the rhythmic unit (example 13).

13

Group 1c: Example, Peteneras

The rhythmic unit of 12 beats can be written as an exchange between 6/8 and 3/4 time. As with the siguiriyas, the eighth-note is the beat (example 14).

14

The rhythmic relationship between these three sub-categories can be seen if, starting with a basic rhythm, the phases of the other two are shifted.

Group 1a: 1 2 3 4 5 6 7 8 9 10 11 12 |1 2 3 4 5 6 7 8 9 10 11 12

Group 1b: 1 2 3 4 5 6 7 8 9 10 11 12

Group 1c: 1 2 3 4 5 6 7 8 9 10 11 12

This shows that the basic rhythmic pattern, repeated in all three groups, is made up of two triple and three double elements.

An intimate knowledge and control of the rhythms, more so than being able to play them with complete exactitude, gives the guitarist that intuitive certainty he needs to take age-old forms and vary and improvise on them to the delight of both himself and his knowledgeable listeners.

Typical Playing Techniques

As has been pointed out, the flamenco guitar was originally used to accompany singers and dancers. Only later did the guitarist's interludes develop into solo performances, which then matured into an independent art form. It was during this maturation process that an increasing number of techniques were borrowed and adapted from classical guitar playing, with the intent of expanding the instrument's expressiveness, especially the melody part and the virtuoso elaboration of chord progressions. However, several characteristics from that original period of accompaniment were retained. For one, the typical playing position: The bottom of the instrument rests on the guitarist's right thigh, with the upper part held just tight enough against his right upper arm to steady the guitar between these two points.

Other characteristics involved the sound, as well as certain techniques used by the left and right hand. In general, the flamenco guitar is played more deliberately and more forcefully. Because of its special structure, the way it is struck, and the (frequent) use of the capo, the voice of the flamenco guitar is dry, a little earthy, and sometimes metallic. This varies of course, depending on how the interpreter conceives his sounds and on the construction of the instrument itself.

Some guitarists have recently tempered this characteristic sound by using instruments that more nearly approach the classical in their material and construction, or even by using amplification.

Flamenco guitar playing differs from classical playing primarily in the use of the following techniques, all of which stem from the period

142

when the guitar was an accompanying instrument: Rasgueado, golpe, apagado and alzapúa.

a) Rasgueado

The Spanish verb "rasguear" means "to stroke" (the strings). So "rasgueado" indicates the "stroking" or striking of whole chords, usually involving five or six strings. There are so many ways of doing this that the guitarist is really only limited by his sense of discovery and invention. Below I have indicated several variants with the usual arrow symbols. The letters p, c, a, m and i indicate the striking finger(s) (see above), while the rhythmic values indicate the relationship between the duration of sound of the individual strokes. An arrow pointed upward means a stroke from the lowest to the highest string, an arrow pointed downward the reverse.

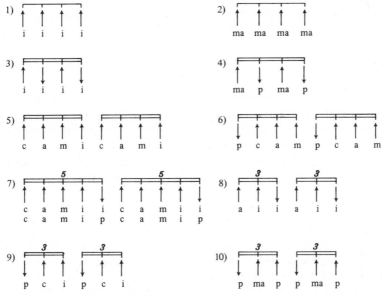

ma = middle and ring fingers strike simultaneously

Examples 5 to 10 illustrate forms that, when combined with speed, perfect rhythm and power, result in a "continuous rasgueado." This means that the individual strokes are no longer audible as such, but give the overall impression of a constant, unbroken roll. This obviously requires persistent study and continued practice.

b) Golpe

An experienced flamenco guitarist ornaments his interpretation with meaningful rhythmic accents. This is done using the technique of *golpe*

(*golpe* = a blow). Golpe is usually executed by rapping with the finger-tip and nail of the ring finger on the harmonic top, which is partially covered with a golpeador (tapping plate) for just this purpose. Here, too, there are many variations: The golpe by itself (e.g. between chords); the golpe at the end of a rasgueado figure; or the golpe together with an index finger rasgueado or thumb stroke. The following shows the rhythm of the rumba flamenca, whose accents are set off by the golpe:

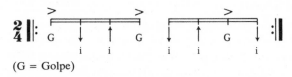

(G = Golpe)

Some guitarists have developed the golpe into a fascinating, at times stupendous display of virtuosity by also tapping the thumb, index finger and outstretched ring finger elsewhere on the surface of the guitar (bridge, edge of the sound hole, side, base of the fingerboard). It should be noted that it is easy for a guitarist to fall into the trap of mere showmanship by resorting to such displays.

c) Apagado

"Apagar" means to dampen. This technique is performed with the little finger (or little finger and ring finger) of the left hand. After a chord has been played, the guitarist immediately damps the strings by placing his outstretched finger(s) across them. This technique can therefore only be used with chords that do not involve the little finger. A similar effect can be achieved by damping a chord with the side of the right hand.

d) Alzapúa

In flamenco guitar, unlike classical, the right thumb is used to play on all strings, even extended melodic passages and arpeggiated chords. Usually played "apoyando," i.e. after playing a string, the thumb ends its stroke against the next string (support stroke). Especially interesting is the use of the thumb nail as a plectrum to pluck either downwards or upwards. This technique is called "alzapúa" (alzar = to raise; púa = plectrum) and can be performed two different ways. But the very distinctive sound is only obtained when the up and downstroke are quite rapid.

Alzapúa on one string:
(tarantas)

Alzapúa on several strings:
Basic pattern:

In addition to the above, most flamenco guitarists (and almost all of those who concertize) now use techniques partially adapted from the repertory of classical guitar: Arpeggio, tremolo in several variants, alternating stroke when playing melodic lines, legato, pizzicato, glissando and harmonics. Clearly, mastering the craft of flamenco guitar requires thorough training, love of music, persistence and plain hard work. In this section I have offered only a glimpse into the fascinating world of flamenco guitar. The following paragraphs may be of interest to those who wish to pursue the subject in somewhat greater depth.

Approaches to Learning the Flamenco Guitar

The best way to learn flamenco guitar has always been to make the acquaintance of singers, dancers and guitarists in their native region of Andalusia or in the large Spanish cities. But this is obviously not possible for most non-Spaniards—except perhaps on an occasional vacation. All the more reason to take advantage of available alternatives, for instance listening to recordings of famous guitarists. I strongly recommend listening to older recordings, as these more closely reflect the original sounds and style of flamenco guitar. I also consider it necessary to familiarize oneself, indeed to immerse oneself in the unique features of flamenco song, its melodies and themes, in order to ensure that one's playing is based on the most thorough comprehension possible. There are exceptionally good recorded anthologies of authentic flamenco music that demonstrate the various movements and personal styles. However, it is still quite difficult to obtain such records (see the Discography, Appendix G).

A good way to improve one's playing is to obtain suitable feedback, to test one's own playing against the standard set by authentic recordings. I thus recommend:

1. Tape recording one's own playing.

2. Playing along with recorded music.

3. Observing one's playing position in the mirror.

The path chosen will obviously be determined by one's own situation and by what one wants to achieve. If already a classical guitar player, is the objective to expand one's repertory with a few playing techniques and flamenco pieces? Alternatively, is the objective to concentrate on flamenco and learn an extensive repertory? If a beginning guitarist, does one wish to study only flamenco? And so on. I would recommend that any beginner start with classical guitar. A thorough knowledge of classical guitar playing and the ability to read music establish a good foundation for playing flamenco guitar. All flamenco guitar methods— even those intended for beginners—move right into the important essentials, i.e. specific playing techniques and solo pieces, to the detriment of technical fine points. But anyone who is gifted and persistent will eventually overcome these hurdles. Today there are many fine method books teaching flamenco guitar (see Appendix).

Flamenco guitar classes are also being offered in major cities around the world, and their numbers have been growing. Periodicals devoted to the guitar and its music are good sources of information about such courses.

As is apparent, any number of opportunities are open to flamenco enthusiasts today, so that anyone seriously interested should not find it too difficult to take the first adventurous steps into this new world. And with growing confidence he will no doubt soon develop his own fresh perspectives.

CASTANETS AND OTHER RHYTHMIC AND PERCUSSIVE ELEMENTS

Ehrenhard Skiera

Song, dance, guitar: This triad comprises the essential elements of flamenco, each of which, on its own, can evoke "duende flamenco," that singular atmosphere and spiritual quality which is the "soul" of flamenco. But there are other components, which, while perhaps not essential, are certainly not unimportant: Playing castanets (called castañuelas or palillos), clapping hands (palmas) and finger snapping (pitos), encouraging shouts by the flamenco artists and the audience (jaleo) during the juerga flamenca, and finally the dancer's rhythmic and percussive footwork (taconeo or zapateado).

Castañuelas or Palillos

The search for the derivation of the word "castanets," leads back to the Spanish words "castaneta" and the more frequently used "castañuelas." Both are related to the Spanish word for chestnut, "castaña." This word, in one idiomatic form or another, has been borrowed from Spanish by almost all other European languages.

Many people assume from the name that castanets were originally made from the wood of chestnut trees or from the nut itself. However, it has been rightly pointed out that neither the wood of the tree nor the chestnut itself are hard enough materials to be made into such an instrument. A better explanation, therefore, lies in their shape itself. The oldest pair of intact castanets suggests the form of a chestnut or other such fruit, and this may have been responsible for the name.

Another term for castanets peculiar to Andalusia is "palillos." Palillos also means "little sticks" and may refer to the practice of rhythmically accompanying song or dance by hitting two sticks together, a practice dating back to ancient Egypt. Another very old form of playing the sticks involved holding two sticks in each hand. One stick was held between the thumb and palm, the other gripped by the four fingers. By slightly opening the hand and snapping it closed, the sticks struck against each other, producing a sharp percussive sound. Distinct pitches could be achieved by changing the angle or the length of the sticks. This was ideal for dancers because it left their arms free for dance movements.

In early Christian times, in the areas around the Aegean and Mediterranean Seas, castanets existed that looked like half-round, angular wooden sticks which were hollowed-out on their flat sides. Two of these were held in one hand. Some were also made out of split bamboo—called in Greek "krotala." These may have an historic connection with the term "palillos." At this very early time, round castanets with a short shaft were also used and were undoubtedly the forerunners of our present-day castanets (see illustration).

Today's castanets consist of two identical, small wooden plates, concave on the inside and similarly rounded on the outside. Both are made from the same piece of wood so that they form an organic whole. Each of the small disks has a fin-shaped handle with two holes in it. The two parts are "hinged" together by a cord threaded through the handle. The castanets can then be played in one hand (usually a pair in each hand) by looping the cord over the thumb.

What Role Do Castanets Play in Flamenco Today?

There are sound reasons for pointing out that castanets do *not* belong to flamenco. They actually inhibit the expressive movement of the hands, which are an integral part of the dance. With few exceptions, they are never used in the baile grande (soleares, siguiriyas, etc.). However, there are many dances in which castanets are used—dances included in the current flamenco repertory, accepting a broad definition of flamenco. In truth all these dances are better classified as Andalusian folk dances than as gypsy flamenco. (Travelers' accounts of the time note that the gypsies of Sacromonte in Granada were using castanets in the 19th century. Was this musical expression based on artistic integrity or a conscious adaptation to what tourists wanted?) It should be remembered that there was a good deal of interplay between baile grande, on the one hand, and Spanish stage dancing and various, popular, regional dances on the other—some of which had always used castanets. The result has been mixed forms that are often difficult to distinguish. What's important, however, is that baile grande was originally danced without castanets, and dancers who care about its origins and about maintaining its stylistic purity do not use castanets in these particular dances. On the other hand, some of the dances known as baile chico would be far less exciting without castanets: The sevillanas, malagueñas, verdiales, fandangos de Huelva and zorongos. These dances are included in the repertories of both classical Spanish stage dancing and flamenco.

Castanets can be sophisticated and extremely expressive rhythmic instruments, but to play them well requires a level of proficiency that is virtually unknown outside Spain; even there it is usually done well only by professional dancers. For this reason I will describe the technique in some detail.

A pair of castanets has two different tones, one brighter, the other fuller. The Spanish call the high castanets "hembra" (little woman) and the low ones "macho" (little man). The castanets are held in place by a cord which is looped over the thumb twice. The knotted end lies over the second thumb joint, with the middle of the cord braced snugly over the cuticle. The "hembra" is played with the right hand, the "macho" the left. When correctly seated, the two halves hang down like slightly parted jaws. Tension on the cord can be regulated by tightening or loosening it. The castanets are suspended from the thumb, which is slightly bent, so that they can be tapped with the fingers. The palms of the hands are turned toward the dancer. Tapping usually involves only the first finger joints, the wrist moving as little as possible. But in general, the dancer's arms, hands and fingers should be relaxed to produce the best and most accurate tone.

Basic Fingering Techniques for the Castanets

Playing the castanets is based on five musical elements: *Tin, tan, tian, carretilla* and *posticeo*. Carretilla and tian are both considered derivative elements, ca-rre-ti-lla being basically a rapid repetition of tin strokes, while tian is tin and tan played together. The table below shows the connections between hands and strokes:

Left hand	Both hands	Right hand
Tan (Ta)	Posticeo (Chapoteo)	Tin (Pi)
	Tian (Pam)	Ca-rre-ti-lla (Rri)

1. Basic stroke: Tin
   Ring and middle finger of the right hand strike the castanets simultaneously.

2. Basic stroke: Tan
   Same as above, with the left hand.

3. Basic stroke: Tian
   Ring finger and middle finger of both hands strike the castanets simultaneously.

4. Basic stroke: Carretilla
   This stroke consists of four even beats in rapid succession with the fingers of the right hand:

   ca = little finger   ti = middle finger
   rre = ring finger   lla = index finger

   When playing a complete rhythm, carretilla is always followed by tan (carretilla = wheelbarrow).

5. Basic stroke: Posticeo, abbreviated Pos
   The two hands are held so that the outer element of the castanets rap against each other. In this movement, the right hand is held a little closer to the body than the left. The castanets hang freely from the thumb and must not be touched by the fingers.

Example of a castanet rhythm in 6/8 time:

A complete history of the castanets, as well as detailed, illustrated playing instructions and progressive exercises for learning the most important rhythms can be found in E. Skiera's *Kastagnettenschule/Method for Castanets*, Apollo-Verlag Paul Lincke, Berlin (in German and English).

Jaleo, Palmas, Pitos, and Taconeo

Although not absolutely necessary, castanets do add a certain richness to the rhythmic accompaniment if used delicately and artistically. Jaleo, palmas, pitos and taconeo, on the other hand, have always been part of flamenco.

The jaleador (*jalear* = to encourage) participates in the juerga either on the stage or from the audience and spurs the artists on with his rhythmic shouts, *palmas* (hand clapping) and *pitos* (finger snapping). "Ole, ole!" (Keep it up! Great!), "así se canta," "así se baila," "así se toca" (That's the way to dance, sing, play!) are calls that help enormously in creating the thrilling, highly-charged atmosphere unique to flamenco, stimulating the singers, dancers and guitarists to give their all. Many jaleadors have almost become virtuosos in the art of palmas. Two or three of them may clap out the rhythms and counter-rhythms with a precision and speed that is indeed breathtaking, while at the same time marking the accents by stamping their feet and clicking their tongues.

By way of example, the basic rhythm pattern of the bulerías consists, as noted in the previous chapter, of twelve beats, with the main accents on 3, 6, 8, 10 and 12. This basic pattern is then frequently overlaid with a double-counted sixth-rhythm with accents on 1, 2 and 4, 5:

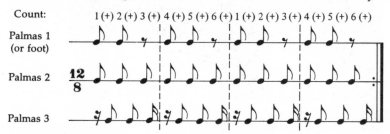

		>		>	>	>		>			
Basic rhythmic pattern:	1 2	3	4	5	6	7	8	9	10	11	12

Basic rhythmic pattern:

```
              >      >  >  >     >
          1 2 3 4 5 6 7 8 9 10 11 12
            >>    >>    >>     >  >
Parallel rhythm:
          1 2 3 4 5 6 1 2 3  4  5  6
```

(These days guitarists usually take their cues from the parallel rhythm and occasionally mark its main accents 1, 2 and 4, 5 with their foot.)

What we call counter-rhythms can then be inserted into these rhythms:

There are two types of palmas, *palmas fuertes* (*fuerte* = strong), in which the fingers of one hand strike the palm of the other, and the *palmas sordas* (*sordo* = muffled, muted), clapping the two slightly cupped palms together to create a muffled sound with more of a bass character. Some cante jondo singers accentuate their own song or the guitarist's preludes and interludes with occasional, soft palmas sordas.

Pitos (finger snapping) has also been developed to a peak of virtuosity. It is usually done with both hands, one marking the basic rhythm, the other the counter-rhythm. And rapidly snapping two or three fingers of one hand sounds something like a carretilla done on the castanets (see above).

Rapping fingers and knuckles on a table top is another way used to create rhythm and percussion, and various shadings of sounds can be achieved. A few flamenco artists have also become virtuosos of this art.

The remaining percussive technique is the *taconeo* (taconear = to stamp with the heel) or zapateado (from zapatear = to stamp with the shoe). Although performed in conjunction with the dance (cf. chapter on the baile), taconeo has an independent musical and rhythmic function. It is, without a doubt, the most impressive percussive element of flamenco. Using tone color (heel, toe, and sole of the shoe), dynamics (loud, soft) and various tempos, as well as by making imaginative use of the entire stage, a talented dancer can create a fascinating, highly diverse "percussive scene" with footwork alone. Taconeo solos are thus part of the repertoire of every cuadro flamenco.

All these techniques require years of practice and—where either dancing or jaleo is concerned—an intuitive feeling for all the various rhythms, not to mention the flamenco lifestyle itself.

FLAMENCOS—PICTURES AND NOTES FROM ANDALUSIA

Holger Mende

Andalusia—Gypsies

Gypsies are found everywhere in Andalusia. The women wear colorful blouses, long skirts and sometimes aprons, large earrings and a carnation in their hair. To earn money they sell carnations, beg, or tell fortunes. The men work at various jobs: Shoeshiners, marketeers, metal work, in swap shops, antique shops, etc. Children work along with their parents from the time they are young. In Fig. 1 a gypsy woman sells cigarettes at the *feria* in Seville.

Trimming a baby's fingernails and toenails is one of the many time-honored rituals among the Andalusian gypsies. It signifies the hope that the young one will grow up to be a successful flamenco singer, dancer or guitar player. Like all Andalusian gypsy rituals, ceremonies and festivals, the "nail fiesta" is celebrated with singing and dancing. Fig. 2 shows singer Antonio Cruz Garcia, known as "Antonio Mairena" (1909–1983) cutting an infant's nails.

Fig. 3 shows Antonio Mairena singing. He is clapping his hands in rhythm to his song. The man behind him wearing glasses is Don Francisco Vallecillo Pecino, who formerly headed the Peña Flamenca in Ceuta (North Africa) and is currently Director of the Flamenco Division in the Andalusian district government in Seville.

Flamenco song, called cante, "emerges" in the truest sense of the word. I heard the most beautiful soleá sung at dawn by the gypsy with the child in Fig. 4. During the Feria de Sevilla a tent city is erected (almost 1,000 tents) among which are always five or six gypsy tents that are—with few exceptions—off limits to non-gypsies. There one hears the best cante, the best guitar playing, and sees the most authentic dancing (Fig. 5). The April feria, where sevillanas (folk dances) are sung and danced day and night, lasts an entire week. Flamenco, which is Andalusian gypsy singing, or simply Andalusian singing—various definitions are now accepted—takes place in intimate settings. The true cante still survives at family gatherings, in the bars and in *ventas* (country inns that are always open).

Figure 1

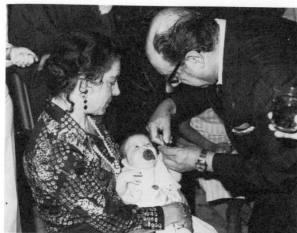

Figure 2

Figure 3

154

Figure 4

Figure 5

I entered a taberna quite by chance, on my way back from a gypsy baptism, to get a cup of coffee. It was 7:00 in the evening. At 9:00 I heard the first "ayaya" of a siguiriya. At 3:00 in the morning the bartender closed the doors after which I heard dozens of songs lasting until the following evening! The cante has not been the exclusive domain of the gypsies for some time now, although they "speak" the cante—as they say in flamenco terminology—with more expressiveness, more sensitivity, more emotion and with greater integrity.

Once in a taberna, after a long conversation, a simple farmer placed his hand on my shoulder (a gesture common to cante, in that cante is a musical message imparted to friends) and sang a soleá.

The cante originated in the provinces of Seville and Cádiz, and today Seville is the center of commercial flamenco. Triana, a part of Seville located on the banks of the Guadalquivir River, was the capital of cante in the 19th century.

The narrow streets and out-of-the-way plazas of the Santa Cruz barrio are overrun with tourists now, but away from all that is the tablao "Los Gallos." Seville has several tablaos, the best of which, in my opinion, is "La Trocha." If one is searching for real cante or a spontaneous juerga, one must go at night to that "other" Seville and simply wait until the cante suddenly erupts from some small group. Many think that flamenco is simply Andalusian folk music, but true flamenco is performed by one person either singing (with only guitar accompaniment) or dancing (but not couples). Andalusian folk dancing and singing, on the other hand, is done in groups.

Whenever gypsies gather for a festive occasion, musical orgies break out. There is song, rhythmic handclapping, guitar playing and improvised dancing to the rhythm of festeros (festive songs), such as tangos, bulerías and alegrías. The visitor can at least get an impression of this kind of gathering by attending one of the many flamenco festivals presented throughout Andalusia during the summer. After five, six, seven, even eight hours of dancing, singing and guitar playing, the final minutes of a festival arrive and all the flamencos who have taken part celebrate the *fin de fiesta* (end of the festival). Each artist, whether singer, dancer, guitarist or palmero, dances a few steps, claps, sings or plays.

Cante

Many of the great singers and guitarists of our century have already passed away: Manuel Torre, Pastora Pavon, known as "La Niña de los Peines," her brother Tomás Pavon, Antonio Mairena and Manolo Caracol. Manuel Ortega Júarez ("Manolo Caracol," 1910–1973) comes from a long line of singers, dancers and bull fighters. He put on pseudo-flamenco shows and used the piano and orchestra to accompany the cante, for which his critics still reproach him. Aside from these aberrations, Caracol was one of the greatest gypsy singers in history.

The man who truly destroyed flamenco was Pepe Marchena. He awed the masses with his 1920s-style tango voice during the dark ages of flamenco in the '40s and '50s. Pictures of both Caracol and Marchena can be seen hanging side by side in many bars in Andalusia.

Fig. 6: Calixto Sánchez Marín ("Calixto Sánchez"), born in 1946 in Mairena del Alcor in the province of Seville, first heard flamenco singing in his father's bar. Flamenco artists who came through Mairena sought out this bar because it was the gathering spot for the local population and the only place where food was served. Calixto Sánchez is one of those artists who can sing virtually any kind of flamenco song. He is a perfectionist and many think his style "cold," for in flamenco, feelings are more important than perfection. A good singer is not necessarily one with a good voice, but someone whose singing makes his listeners "suffer." As a grade school teacher, Calixto occupies a special place among flamencos. This is also true of the guitarist Pedro Peña, who also

Figure 6

teaches primary school, and of Alfredo Arrebolo, who teaches at the University of Málaga. José Menese Scott, known as "José Menese," was born in 1942 in Puebla de Cazalla in the province of Seville and was a shoemaker before he took up cante. He is one of the most versatile singers of the younger generation. He is a master of the martinetes, which belong to the family of toñas and are sung without any accompaniment.

Fernanda Jiménez Peña ("Fernanda de Utrera"), born in 1923, is the best soleá singer living today and follows in the long tradition of female singers from La Andonda to La Serneta. No recording can really do justice to her expressive voice. She always appears with her sister Bernarda, who in turn is one of the best bulería interpreters. Their family has produced a number of flamencos. They are gypsies and related to Peña of Lebrija.

José Domingues Muñoz ("El Cabrero") was born in 1944 in Aznalcollar in the province of Seville and is one of the more exotic figures in the flamenco world. He comes from a very poor family and is a goatherd. He spent his youth herding goats and later became part of "La Cuadra," a theater group in Seville. He sings protest songs, an unconventional genre for flamenco. José is the hero of Andalusia's farm workers and all hell breaks loose wherever he makes an appearance. He always wears a dark, broad-brimmed hat, a red scarf, a black shirt and black boots. He lives near Seville with a Swiss woman and their four children and keeps a herd of almost 400 goats.

Juan Fernández Peña ("El Lebrijano") was born in 1941 in Lebrija in the province of Seville. A blond gypsy, he is a member of the famous Peña dynasty. He ranks as one of the finest contemporary gypsy singers. His mother is the famous singer Maria Peña ("La Perrata"), and his brother the famous guitarist Pedro Peña.

Antonio Nuñez Montoya ("Chocolate") was born in 1931 in Jerez de la Frontera in the province of Cádiz. Chocolate is a gypsy and the greatest living siguiriya singer, as well as one of the last true flamencos. He has his own unique philosophy and composes poetry, though he cannot write (like so many of the anonymous Andalusian poets).

He once said to me, "I came to flamenco from abject poverty. No one who has not experienced such wretchedness and persecution can really understand our people—the gypsies—or flamenco. Only someone who has grown up with sorrow can sing flamenco. I know only sadness, and even if I am sometimes happy, this core of sadness never leaves me."

Today Chocolate lives in a modest apartment in Seville with his wife Rosa, sister of the famous gypsy dancer Antonio Montoya Flores ("El Farruco").

Fig. 7: The gypsy singer Rancapino from Chiclana in the province of Cádiz, here accompanied by the guitarist Manolo Dominguez, also known as "El Rubio." Rancapino is one of the best singers from Cádiz province. His beautiful voice is mellow and slightly guttural. Like all gypsies, he learned his first cantes from his parents, grandparents or other relatives. The picture illustrates the deep physical and emotional involvement of a good cante singer, one who makes his listeners "suffer," i.e., participate in the song with their emotions as well as their minds.

Fig. 8: The guitarist plays a few falsetas during a pause in the cante, while Rancapino quietly claps the palmas to keep the song's compás (beat, measure, rhythm). Compás is everything in true cante and nobody has mastered it like the gypsies. The reason there are so few non-gypsies (payos) who sing the bulería is probably because its compás is extremely complex.

Fig. 9: Francisco Garrasco ("Curro Malena") was born in 1945 and is another gifted singer from Lebrija in the province of Seville. Lebrija is one of those southern Andalusian towns that has produced generations of singers, dancers and guitarists. Curro Malena numbers among the *cantaores largos* (singers who have mastered many types of songs), as contrasted to *cantaores cortes* (those able to sing only a few). But he is best known for his fantastic interpretations of soleáres and bulerías. Like many others, he refuses to work in tablaos, for "in those places the purity of the song vanishes." But for many artists, tablaos are the only way of getting work; they also serve as an avenue into commercial flamenco, which is well paid. Curro spends a few months a year in Lebrija to drink from the wellspring of genuine cante: The cante of the gypsies.

Fig. 10: Flamenco as a form of musical expression no longer belongs exclusively to southern Andalusian gypsies. Ever since Silverio Franconetti Aguilar (1831–1889) took flamenco singing out of the privacy of the gypsy family and put it on the stages of the cafés cantantes, more and more payo artists have joined the ranks of performers. There are now as many payo flamencos as gypsy, even though the experts still say only gypsies possess the authentic song, with its severe

Figure 7

Figure 8

Figure 9

melancholy and deeply emotional quality. One of the best payo
flamenco singers today is José Sanchez Bernal. He was born in Seville in
1933 and sings under the sobriquet "Naranjito de Triana." He is also a

Figure 10

Figure 11

notable guitarist and guitar maker. He lives in Seville on a street named Jiménez de Enciso, only a few yards away from guitarist José Luis Postigo's shop. Naranjito is one of the greatest authorities on flamenco in the last 50 years.

Fig. 11: Antonio Montoya Flores, born in 1916 and known as "El Farruco," comes from a Canastero family (transient gypsies) and is one of the best dancers now performing. Flamencos are special people and many are camera shy. Farruca gave me this staged picture—the type, rather "kitschy," that is still being made all over Andalusia.

Baile

Dance schools in Andalusia are booked solid and many of the students are foreigners. However, true flamenco dancing is not choreographed. Farruco once said to me: "What do I dance on the stage? I never know beforehand. It depends on what I feel like, on my mood." When asked what he teaches his students, he answered, "I improvise."

Manuela Carrasco, who was born in 1958, is one of today's most promising young dancers.

Toque

Pedro Peña ("Pedro Bacan") was born in 1951 in Lebrija in the province of Seville. He is probably the most versatile, creative and brilliant guitarist now performing in Andalusia. This "gentle giant" is a true authority on flamenco culture. He has taught flamenco guitar at American universities and now directs a group of flamenco guitarists of various degrees of advancement in Alcalá de Guadaira. Peña is a gypsy married to an American from Denver; they have two sons and live in San Juan de Aznal arache near Seville. Pedro contends that flamenco guitar playing cannot be learned by practicing alone in a room, that it needs the human element, namely a singer. Although Pedro cannot read music, he has created his own notation using numbers. In his opinion, all the published methods of teaching flamenco guitar are useless. In the company of other guitarists and a music teacher from Alcalá, we discussed about 20 different methods, but he believes that flamenco cannot be rendered by notes on a page.

Like many flamencos, José Luis Postigo Guerra (born in 1950 in Seville) first started as a dancer, taking up the guitar when he was 15. Since then he has become one of the best flamenco accompanists. Postigo, like most flamenco guitarists, does not read music and has never studied harmony. He also builds and sells guitars from his small workshop.

Francisco López-Cepero García ("Paco Cepero"), born in 1942 in Jerez de la Frontera in the province of Cádiz, is just the opposite of Postigo. Today there are three different approaches to guitar playing: (1) As pure accompaniment to song, that is, subordinated to it—the true purpose of flamenco guitar; (2) guitar accompaniment, but accompaniment that overpowers the song with its display of virtuosity—long, complicated falsetas, lengthy openings, emphasis on thumbwork, etc.; and (3) flamenco guitar as a solo instrument. Cepero belongs to the second group.

There are many guitarists who claim to have studied under the famous "Diego del Gastor," but his only serious student was his nephew, "Paco del Gastor."

Cabales and Aficionados

The Cátedra de Flamencologia y Estudies Folklóricos Andaluces is in Jerez de la Frontera, in the province of Cádiz, a place where, it is said, even the stones sing. The Cátedra was founded in 1958; its purpose is to house and preserve all documents about flamenco and Andalusian folklore, to study the origins, influences, evolution, variants, etc. of

Figure 12

flamenco (cante, baile and toque), and to assemble books, music scores, photographs, art objects, records and tapes.

One of its main purposes is to protect folklore and flamenco against impurities and declining standards and to increase public awareness of flamenco culture. Throughout the year the Cátedra offers lectures and sponsors evenings of song, dance and guitar playing. It awards prizes and has its own publishing house. In the summer it offers international summer courses, attended by students from all over the world, as well as from Spain, who come to learn to dance, play the guitar and even to sing. These classes are supplemented by lectures on every aspect of flamenco. However, the Cátedra is not held in high regard by either gypsy or payo flamenco connoisseurs.

My friend José Romero, the flamenco pianist, admits that he is a member of the Cátedra, but says that they "do nothing." Most peñas (clubs) flamencas are run by payos. I have only seen one genuine gypsy peña, in Puerto de Santa Maria in Cádiz province, and on the door hung a sign, "Members Only." The gypsies obviously do not care for outsiders. I once was with a friend at a peña flamenca where payos were appearing, and during the performance my friend leaned over to me and whispered, "How coldly they sing, they don't have any jondo."

Figure 13

Fig. 12: Many peñas hold dance classes. This young girl of 13 is learning flamenco dancing.

At first, the only accompaniment to flamenco was rhythmic; the guitar was introduced as an accompanying instrument only in the 19th century. And even though in the last 50 years flamenco has been danced and sung to orchestras, organs, flutes, etc., guitar music still remains the most authentic form of accompaniment.

Fig. 13: José Romero Jiménez, born in 1936 in Osuna in the province of Seville, is the best flamenco pianist in the world. He alone has succeeded in drawing the feeling of jondo (depth) from the piano. In addition to being a pianist, Romero teaches at a school in Seville, and has written several books on Andalusian music. His records include: *El Piano Flamenco* (Hispavox), *Andalucia Flamenca en el Piano de José Romero* (Hispavox), *Formas Musicales Andaluzas* (Zafiro), and *Formas Musicales Andaluzas y Formas Libre* (Zafiro). Romero has been the recipient of several awards, including the Premio Nacional de Flamencología in 1976. He is a member of the Cátedra de Flamencología in Jerez. In my opinion, Romero is the outstanding authority on the art of flamenco, yet he remains practically unknown outside Spain.

APPENDIXES

A. Flamenco Festivals

Guide to Spanish flamenco festivals: *Guia de Festivales Flamenco,* an annual published by: Junta de Andalucia, Consejeria de Cultura, Departamento de Flamenco.

Benalmadena: Festival Alay
Bornos: Berza flamenca, August
Cabra: Flamenco Cayetano Muriel "Niña de Cabra," September
Cabra: Romeria Nacional de Gitanos, June
Cartagena: Concursos de Cartageneras
Cordoba: Patios Cordobeses
Granada: As part of the International Music Festival, June/July
Jerez de la Frontera: F.de Espana de arte flamenco y cursos de Flamencología, August/September
Jerez de la Frontera: Fiesta de la Bulería, June
La Union: Festival cante de las minas
Lebrija: Caracola
Lucena: Noche flamenca del campo andaluz, July
Mairena del Alcor: Festival Antonio Mairena
Málaga: Moraga flamencas
Morón de la Frontera: Gazpacho andaluz
Puente genil: Festival del Cante grande
Sevilla: part of the Feria de abril
Utrera: Potaje gitano

There are other festivals in Tarifa (September), Sanlucar de Barrameda (August), Ronda (September), San Roque, Fuengirola, Bajadoz and Madrid.

For festivals in U.S. a good source of information is:

Paco Sevilla
P.O. 4706
San Diego, CA 92104
Tel: (619) 282-2837

B. Peñas ("Clubs") flamencas

Algeciras: Sociedad del Cante Grande, Huerta Ancha No. 3
Almeria: Peña "El Taranto", Tenor Iribane No. 10
Archidonia: Peña flamenca Carrera No. 42/2
Avila: Peña "Don Antonio Chacón", Vasco de Quiroga No. 1
Bajadoz: Asociación de Arte flamenco, Apartado No. 150
Barcelona: Peña flamenca "Enrique Morrente", Viladrana No. 100
Cádiz: Peña "El Mellizo", Paseo S. Felipe
Ceuta: Tertulia flamenca de Ceuta, Plaza Teniente Ruiz No. 3
Cordoba: Peña flamenca "Aleczar Viejo", Puerta de Sevilla No. 1
Fuente de Cantos: Peña flamenca "Curro Malena", P. Manjon X No. 1
Granada: Peña "La Plateria", Placeta de Toqueros No. 3
Jerez de la Frontera: "Peña flamenca Jerezana", Merced No. 16 "Centro cultural flamenco D. Antonio Chacon", Carmen No. 24
Hillsboro, Oregon: La Zambra, Studio of José and Diana Solano; professional artists gather for juergas.
Lebrija: Federacion Provincal de entidades flamencas, Callejon de los Frailes
Madrid: Peña flamencofíla universitaria "Silverio", Colégio Mayor Santiago Apostol, Donoso Cortes No. 63
Peña Menese, Trafalgar No. 4 (Mesón Jerezano) Coslada––M.
Málaga: Peña "Juan Breva", Callejon del Picaor No. 2
Montalban de Cordoba: Peña "Los Cabales del Cante", Ancho No. 57
Osuna: Tertulia flamenca de Osuna, Eduardo Callejo No. 1
Puerto de Santa Maria: Tertulia flamenca Portuense, Zarza No. 42
Sevilla: Peña cultural flamenca "Manuel Vallejo", Guadal Canal No. 2, Local 5
Velez-Málaga: Peña flamenca "Niño de Velez", Calle Tejada/Edif. Granada bajo
Federación de Peñas flamencas: D. Antonio Nuñez Romero (Pres.), c/Caracuel No. 17, Radio Jerez, Jerez de la Frontera

(Further information can be obtained from local tourist offices.)

Clubs and Societies in the U.S.

A good source of information is the *North American Flamenco Directory* published by the Flamenco Association of San Diego, Box 4706, San Diego, CA 92104.

C. Flamenco Research Centers

Centro de Estudios de Música Andaluza de Flamenco Madrid, Avenida de los Reyes Catolicos, 4
Cátedra de Flamencología y Estudios Folkloricos Andaluzes Jerez de la Frontera, c/Quintos, Tel. 349702
Museo del Arte Flamenco Jerez de la Frontera, Plaza de San Marcos, 14
Centro de Actividades Flamencas Mario Maya, Sevilla, Pasaje Mallol 20
Estudios Flamencos José Heredia Maya, Universidad de Granada, Granada

Workshops and Classes in the U.S.

Given at various times in many cities throughout the U.S. The Arte Flamenco Dance Company offers workshops (Rt. 1, Box 664, Hillsboro, OR 97123) at their studio, in Portland, and other locations. An annual summer workshop, followed by juergas, is directed by the flamenco dancer Teo Morca at his academy, 1349 Franklin St., Bellingham, WA 98225.

D. Suppliers of Sheet Music, Records, Books

Society of Spanish Studies, Victor Pradera, 46, Madrid
Ivor Mairants Musicentre, London

E. Flamenco Guitar Instruction Guides

In Spanish:

Rafael Morales: *Método de Guitarra,* Granada 1954 (Ediciones Sacromonte, in notation and tablature)
Emilio Medina: *Método de Guitarra Flamenca,* Buenos Aires 1958 (Ricordi)
Andres Batista: *Método de Guitarra Flamenca,* Madrid 1979 (Union Musical Española, in notation and tablature)

Alfonso Puig Claramunt, *El Arte del Baile Flamenco.* Ediciones Poligrapha, S.A., Barcelona [n.d.]—contains basic exercises, historical information on Flamenco dance, excellent photos.

In English:

Ivor Mairants: *Flamenco-Guitar,* London 1958 (Latin-American Music Publishing Co., notation and tablature, with a record by Pepe del Sur)
Juan D. Grecos: *The Flamenco Guitar,* New York 1973 (Sam Fox Publishing Co., outstanding teaching text in notation and tablature)
Juan Martin: *El Arte Flamenco de la Guitarra,* London 1978 (United Music Publishers Ltd, very thorough work in notation and tablature, with cassette)

A basic course of instruction in Flamenco guitar consisting of audio casettes and sheet music is available from

> Mariano Cordoba
> 647 E. Garland Terrace
> Sunnyvale, CA 94086

There is an enormous amount of sheet music available for flamenco guitar, but the beginner should be very careful in using it, as the notation can be unreliable. Ricordi Verlag (Munich) in Germany has extensive offerings. Many other publishers throughout the world also sell flamenco music.

F. Addresses of Famous Flamenco Guitar Makers

José Ramirez II, Concepción Jeronima 2, Madrid
Conde Hermanos, Gravina 7, Madrid
Manuel Contreras, Calle Mayor 80, Madrid
Manuel Reyes, Plaza del Potro 2, Córdoba
Miguel Rodriguez, Alfaros 15, Córdoba

When purchasing a flamenco guitar, it is best to obtain the advice of a native tocaor.

Flamenco guitar makers in the U.S.:
>John Shelton Susan Farreta
>5031 S.E. 115th
>Portland, OR 97266

>Lester De Voe
>2436 Renfield Way
>San José, CA 95148

>Manuel A. Rodriguez
>3455 Birch St.
>Denver, CO 80207

G. Discography

Dance

Carmen Amaya "In Memoriam" Brunswick	LPBM 87 700
José Greco "Flamenco rhythms"	Everest 3216
La Joselito	LDM 4214
Lucero Tena "Palillos Flamencos"	Vogue LVLXHS 8830

Zambra (with Rosa Durán, Paco el Laberinto) Fontana 858 091 FPY
Olé! Festival Flamenco Gitano (with Caraestaca, El Guito, La Singla, La Tati)
Philips 843977 PY

Guitar

Manuel Cano "Evocación de la guitarra de Ramón Montoya"	Hispavox HH 10-252
Mario Escudero	ABC-Paramount 396
Diego el del Gastor "Misterios de la guitarra flamenca"	Ariola 10521
Roman el Granaino "Guitare flamenco"	Le chant du monde LDX 74367

Perico del Lunar "Guitariste flamenco"	BAM LD 362
Paco de Lucia "Fuente y Caudal"	Philips 6328109
Melchor de Marchena "Guitarra Gitana"	Hispavox HH 10-151
Pepe Martinez "Guitarra Flamenca"	Hispavox HH 10-152
Ramón Montoya "Arte clasico Flamenco"	BAM LD 430
Paco Peña	Fontana 6438 011
Niño Ricardo "Toques Flamencos"	Hispavox HH 1049
Niño Ricardo "Guitare Flamenco"	Le chant du monde LDM 4045
José Pisa "Le nouveau monde du flamenco"	Pathé C 062-11821
Sabicas "Flamenco puro"	Hispavox 130 076
Sabicas "El rey del Flamenco	Fontana 701 551 WPY
Serranito "El Flamenco en la guitarra de Victor Monge Serranito"	Hispavox HH 10-291

Vocal

Anthologies

Antologia del Cante Flamenco	Hispavox HH 1.201-2-3
Antologia del Cante Flamenco y Cante Gitano	Decca 258.031-32-33
Antologia de los Cantes de Cádiz	Hispavox 10-193
Archivo del Cante Flamento	Vergara 13001-SJ/13006-SJ
Canta Jerez	Hispavox HH 10-341
Cunas del Cante: Vol 1 Los Puertos	Clave 18-1295
Cunas del Cante: Vol 2 Jerez	Clave 18-1310
Flamencos de Jerez	CBS S-64244
La gran historia del cante gitano andaluz (Antonio Mairena)	Columbia MCE 814/816
Una historia del Cante Flamenco (Manolo Caracol)	Hispavox HH 10-23/24
Sevilla Cuna del cante flamenco	Columbia CCLP 31008
Tesoros del Flamenco Antiguo (Pepe el de la Matrona)	Hispavox HH 10-346/47

Historic Recordings

Colección de Cantes Flamencos (including A. Chacon, M. Torre, J. Breva, J. Mojama)	Audio A-10014
Los ases del Flamenco: Don Antonio Chacon	EMI C 038-021 511
Los ases del Flamenco: José Cepero/	EMI C 038-021 520
Los ases del Flamenco: Tómas Pavon/	EMI C 038-021 628
Los ases del Flamenco: Manuel Torre/ El Tenazas de Moron	EMI C 038-021 510
Niña de Los Peines	EMI 1 J 040 20.077M

Recordings of Individual Artists

El Agujetas: Cantes gitanos de Manuel Agujetas	Ariola 82158-H
El Agujetas: Cien años atras	CFE P1974
El Agujetas: Viejo Cante Jondo	CBS S-64216
Tio Borrico de Jerez	RCA SPBO-2208
Manolo Caracol: Cante Grande	RCA LSP-10464
El Chocolate	Clave 18-1160
Fosforito	Philips 843 145 PY
Antonio Mairena: La llave de oro del Cante Flamenco	Hispavox HH 10-251
Antonio Mairena: Cien años de Cante Gitano	Hispavox HH 10-269
Curro Mairena: Los duendes de Curro Mairena	Movie Play S-21.300
Pepe el de la Matrona	BAM LD 342
José Menese	RCA CAS 10 169
José Menese: Cantes Flamencos Basicos	RCA 10340
José el Negro	Movie Play 13.0854/9
Tia Anica la Piriñaca: 4 veces veinte años	RCA PL-35 136
Rafael Romero	BAM LD 361
Aurelio Selle	Hispavox HH 10-194
Terremoto de Jerez: Genio y duende del Cante Gitano	Hispavox HH 10-361
Terremoto de Jerez: Homenaje a Terremoto de Jerez	Hispavox 157 001
Juan Talega: Una reliquia del Cante Gitano	Columbia SCGE 81 172
Fernanda y Bernarda de Utrera	Hispavox HHS 10-379

H. Glossary

aficionado	connoisseur, fan
agitanado	assimilated by gypsies
alzapúa	thumb technique for the guitar
apoyando	guitar playing technique
aspazo	to mute (guitar)
baile	the dance
bailaor/bailaora	dancer
bata de cola	typical flamenco dress
braceo	arm movements during the dance
cabales	persons initiated into flamenco
caló	language of the gypsies
café cantante	cafe with musical performances (1860–1910)
cantaor/cantaora	singer
cante	song
cante alante	song without dance
cante atrás	song with/to a dance
cante campero	songs with rural themes and origins
cante chico	light song
cante festero	festive song
cante grande = jondo	serious, "deep" song
cante intermedio	song between jondo and chico
cante jondo (hondo)	profound, meaningful song
cante para bailar	song to a dance
cante para escuchar	song sung for listening only
cantañuelas	castanets
ceijilla	capo (guitar)
compás	beat, rhythm
concurso	competition
copla	verse (temple/salida, tercios/caida)
cuadro	group of flamenco artists
duende	ghost, demon or spirit in folk music and dancing
escobillo	turn executed with the train of a dress
falseta	variations on the guitar
feria	town or district festival
gitano	Spanish gypsy
gitanería	gypsy quarter
golpe	rhythmic accentuation (guitar)
intermedio	intermediate (between serious and light song)
jaleador	mood setter
jaleo	encouraging words
jipío	cry, lament
juerga	spree, gathering of aficionados to enjoy music and drink
macho	final song passages

mozarabic	influenced by the Moors
palillo	small stick for keeping rhythm (castanets)
palmas	rhythmic hand clapping
a palo (seco)	accompanied by style stick
payo	non-gypsy
pito	finger snapping
punteado	each note plucked separately (guitar)
rasgueado	strumming of chords (guitar)
remate	final song
reunión	private flamenco party
roma	Romanichal, gypsy race
tablao	low stage for performances
taconeo	heel tapping
temple	vocalization, warm-up
tercio	section or part of song
tocaor	guitarist
toque	flamenco played on guitar
valiente	having a powerful voice
voz afillá	rasping vocal style
voz fácil	fresh, facile vocal style
voz naturá	natural vocal register
voz redonda = redonda	male vocal register
zapateado	heel and foot stamping

BIBLIOGRAPHY

Alvarez Caballero, Angel: *Historia del Cante Flamenco,* Madrid 1981.

Bloch, Jules: *Les Tsiganes,* Paris 1969.

Beaumont, Cyril Williams Antonio: *Impressions of the Spanish Dancer,* London, A. & C. Black, 1952.

Blume, Friedrich (ed.): *Die Musik in Geschichte und Gegenwart* (MGG) Kasel/Basel 1955 ff. (Vol. 4: Flamenco, Vol. 5: Guitar).

Borrow, George Zincali: *An Account of the Gypsies in Spain,* London, John Murray, 1901.

Brown, Irving Henry: *Deep Song: Adventures with Gypsy Songs and Singers in Andalusia and Other Lands,* N.Y. & London, Harper and Bros., 1929.

_____ : *Nights and Days on the Gypsy Trail,* N.Y. and London, Harper & Bros., 1922.

Brunelleschi, Elsa: *Antonio and Spanish Dancing,* London, A. & C. Black, 1958.

Caba, Pedro y Carlos: *Andalucia, su comunismo y su cante jondo,* Madrid 1933.

Caballero Bonald, José María: *Archivo del cante flamenco,* Barcelona 1969.

_____ : *Luces y sombras del flamenco,* Barcelona 1975.

Cadalso, José: *Cartas marruecas,* Madrid 1975.

Cansinos Assens, Rafael: *La copla andaluza,* Madrid 1976.

Clébert, Jean-Paul: *Los gitanos,* Barcelona 1965.

Cobo, Eugenio: *Pasión y muerte de Gabriel Macandé,* Madrid 1977.

de Falla, Manuel: *Escritos sobre música y músicas,* Madrid 1972.

_____ : *On Music and Musicians,* London, Marion Boyars, 1979.

Díaz del Moral, Juan: *Historia de las agitaciones campesinas andaluzas,* n.p., n.d.

Drillon, Lilyana et al.: *Quejio: Informe,* Madrid 1975.

Dumas, Danielle: *Coplas Flamencas,* Paris 1973.

García Lorca, Federico: *Obras completas,* Madrid 1973.

_____ : *Teoria y juego del duende,* in: *Obras Completas,* Madrid 1967.

_____ : *Poem of the Deep Song,* City Lights Books, San Francisco 1987.

Garcia Ulecia, Alberto: *Las confesiones de Antonio Mairena,* Sevilla 1976.

George, David: *The Flamenco Guitar,* Society of Spanish Studies, Madrid 1969.

_____ : *The Flamenco Guitar: from Its Birth in the Hands of the Guitarrero to Its Ultimate Celebration in the Hands of the Flamenco Guitarist,* Madrid, Society of Spanish Studies, 1969.

Gerena, Manuel: *Cantes del pueblo—para el pueblo,* Barcelona 1975.

Gobin, Alain: *Le Flamenco,* Paris 1975.

Gómez, Agustín: *El Neoclasicismo flamenco,* Cordoba 1978.

González Climent, Anselmo: *Flamencología,* Madrid 1964.

_____ : *Pepe Marchena y la opera flamenca y otros ensayos,* Madrid n.d.

Grande, Felix: *Memoria del flamenco,* 2 vol., Madrid 1979.

Greco, Jose: *The Gypsy in My Soul: The Autobiography of Jose Greco,* N.Y., Doubleday & Co., 1977.

Grelmann, G.H.M.: *Geschichte der Zigeuner,* Leipzig 1783.

Grunfeld, J.: *Manuel de Falla: Spanien und die neue Musik,* Zürich 1968.

Hecht, Paul: *The Wind Cried: An American's Discovery of the World of Flamenco,* N.Y. Dial Press, 1968.

Heredia Maya, José: *Camelamos naquerar,* Granada 1976.

_____ : *Peñar Ocono,* Granada 1974.

_____ : Interview in *Ideal,* Granada.

Howson, Gerald: *The Flamencos of Cádiz Bay,* London, Hutchinson, 1965.

Jung, Christof: *Die Interpreten des Cante Flamenco,* Mainz 1974.

_____ : *Flamenco-Lieder,* Köln 1970.

Kuckertz, Josef: *Musik in Asien I. Indien und der vordere Orient,* Kassel 1981.

Larrea, Arcadio: *El Flamenco en su ráiz,* Madrid 1974.

Liégeois, Jean-Pierre: *Les Tsiganes,* Paris 1971.

Machado y Alvarez, Antonio ("Demófilo"): *Colección de cantes flamencos,* Madrid 1975.

Mairants, Ivor: *The Flamenco Guitar: A Complete Method for Playing Flamenco Music on the Spanish Guitar, Suitable for the Beginner, the Advanced Player and the Teacher,* London, Latin-American Music Publishing Co., 1958.

Martin, Juan: *Guitar Method, El arte flamenco de la guitarra,* London 1978.

Meudtner, Ilse: Flamenco Showgeschäft und Wirklichkeit, in: *Merian* 5 XXX/C.

Mindling, Roger: *Spanischer Tanz,* Olten 1966.

Molina, Ricardo: *Misterios del arte flamenco,* Barcelona 1967.

_____ : *Obra flamenca,* Madrid 1977.

Molina, Ricardo y Mairena, Antonio: *Mundo y formas del cante flamenco,* Granada/Sevilla 1971.

Moreno Casado, José: *Los gitanos desde su penetración en España su condición social y jurídica,* Granada 1949.

The New Grove Dictionary of Music and Musicians, S. Sadie (ed.), Washington, 1980, art. "Flamenco".

Niles, Doris: *El Duende,* N.Y. Dance Perspectives, 1966.

Ortíz Nuevo, José Luis (ed.): *Las mil y una historia de Pericón de Cádiz,* Madrid 1975.

Pepe El de la Matrona: *Recuerdos de un cantaor sevillano,* Madrid 1975.

Perez, Manuel L.: *Pueblo y Politico en el C. Jondo,* Sevilla 1980.

Pohren, Donn: *The Art of Flamenco,* Madrid, 1962, 3rd ed. 1972 (see below).

_____ : *Lives and Legends of Flamenco: A Biographical History,* Madrid/Sevilla 1964.

_____ : *L'art flamenco,* Sevilla 1962.

_____ : *The Art of Flamenco,* 3rd ed., Moron de la Frontera, Society of Spanish Studies, 1972.

Pott, A. F.: *Die Zigeuner in Europa und Asien,* Halle 1944/45.

Puig Claramunt, Alfonso: *El arte de baile flamenco,* Barcelona 1977.

_____ : *El arte del baile flamenco,* Barcelona, Ediciones poligrafa, S.A., publication date not given (in German, French, Spanish and English).

Quiñones, Fernando: *El flamenco, Vida y muerte,* Barcelona 1971.

_____ : *De Cádiz y sus cantes,* Madrid 1975.

Ramírez, Heredia: *Juan de Dios, Vida gitana,* Barcelona 1973.

Riesenfeld, Janet: *Dancer in Madrid,* Funk & Wagnalls Co., N.Y. and London, 1938.

Ríos Ruíz, Manuel: *Introducción al cante flamenco,* Madrid 1976.

Rishi, W. R.: *Roma,* Delhi 1976.

San Román, Teresa: *Vecinos gitanos,* Madrid 1976.

Sánchez Ortega, María Helena: *Documentación selecta sobre la situación de los gitanos españoles en el siglo XVIII,* Madrid 1977.

Sarraute, Claude: La Joselito, au Petit-Odéon, in: *Le Monde,* Paris, June 1967.

Starkie, Walter: *Auf Zigeuner-Spuren,* München 1957.

_____ : Spain: *A Musician's Journey Through Time and Space,* vol. II, pt. 3: The Gypsy Journey, E.D.I.S.L.I., Geneva, 1958, p. 95–96.

Touma, Habib Hassan: Die Musik der Araber im 19.Jahrhundert, in: *Musikkulturen Asiens, Afrikas und Ozeaniens im 19.Jahrundert,* Regensburg 1973.

El de Triana, Fernando: *Arte y artistas flamencos,* Madrid 1935.

Udaeta, José: *Flamenco,* Hamburg 1964.

Vaux de Foletier, François de: *Mil años de historia de los gitanos,* Barcelona 1973.

Vossen, Rüdiger: *Zigeuner,* Frankfurt/M./Berlin 1983.

Periodicals:

Flamenco. Published and edited by: Detlev Eberwein, Hohenstr. 11, D-8752 Geiselbach, West Germany.

Jaleo. Journal published by the Flamenco Association of San Diego, Box 4706, San Diego, CA 92104.

ABOUT THE AUTHORS

Madeleine Claus, Ph.D., lives in Banyuls (southern France) and was introduced to flamenco by her husband, the flamenco guitarist Pedro Solér. She and Solér's sister Isabel are putting together a collection of flamenco records, books and video cassettes in Toulouse. Her many trips to Spain and her close friendship with many flamenco artists, such as "La Joselito" have helped deepen her knowledge of flamenco. Madeleine Claus is currently working on a biography of "La Joselito."

Christof Jung is a bookseller in Mainz and a specialist in flamenco. Jung lived with the gypsies in Andalusia for many months and has published several works on flamenco, especially on cante (*Die Interpreten des Cante Flamenco, Nanas-Wiegenlieder, Die Flamenco-Lieder,* etc.)

Holger Mende has lived for many years in Seville and is a flamenco aficionado. He has thus been able to observe first-hand what is currently happening in gypsy-Andalusian flamenco. Because Mende knows many flamenco artists personally, he has been able to enrich this book with "living histories."

Marion Papenbrok, Ph.D., lives in Eppelheim near Heidelberg. Her doctoral dissertation was a comparison of Artaud's "Theater of Cruelty" with flamenco. She has travelled to Andalusia several times to do research and has published works on flamenco and on the gypsies.

Bernhard-Friedrich Schulze teaches music and other subjects at the Modellschule Obersberg in Bad Hersfeld. In 1973 he studied flamenco guitar under Francisco Solér-Lopez in Málaga. Since that time he has continued his studies of flamenco guitar. In the summer of 1984 he studied in Madrid and Andalusia.

Ehrenhard Skiera, Ph.D. in musicology and theory of education, teaches at the University of Giessen, where he also lectured on flamenco guitar. Many research trips to Andalusia and Madrid. Numerous publications on guitar: *Flamenco-Gitarrenschule* (1973). Various guitar methods: *Klingender Lehrgang für Flamenco-Gitarre* (1980), as well as editions of classical and modern guitar music.

SPAIN

PORTUGAL

FRANCE

La Coruña · Villalba · Gijón · Ribadesella · Llanes · Unquerra · Altamira · Santander
· Santiago · Oviedo · Santillana · San Sebastian
Sangenjo · Pontevedra · Puente-Viesgo **Bilbao** · Vitoria · Pamplona · Berdún · Cadaques
· Vigo · Orense · Villafranca · León · Osorno · Tossa de mar · Lloret de mar
· Verin
· Zamora · Valladolid · Soria · Ricla · Zaragoza **Barcelona**
· Salamanca · Rueda · Segovia · Castellote
· Avila · Escorial · Peñiscola
· Béjar **Madrid** · Castellón de la Plana **Palma**
Tagus · Toledo · Cuenca **Valencia** **Ibiza** **Malorca**
· Cáceres · Belmonte · Altea · Calpe · Villajoyosa **Formentera**
Lisbon · Merida · Agudo · Manzanares · Elche **Alicante**
· Badajoz · Calzada **Murcia**
Cordoba · Linares · Lorca
Guadalquivir · Jaén · Cartagena
Alcalá del Rio **ANDALUSIA**
Cartaya · Huelva **Seville** · Archidona · Loja · Guadix · Granada · Almeria
Jerez de la Frontera · Arcos de la Frontera **Malaga**
· Cádiz · Ronda
Gibraltar (Great Britain) _Mediterranean Sea_

North Atlantic Ocean

Strait of Gibraltar

MOROCCO